# The Evolution of Catholic Unbelief

## Thomas L. McFadden

## Institute for Science and Catholicism

i

Email: SCIENCEandCATHOLICISM@GMAIL.COM.
On the web: www.ScienceAndCatholicism.org
On Facebook: Institute for Science and Catholicism

**Library Cataloging Data**

*The Evolution of Catholic Unbelief* by Thomas L. McFadden
BISAC: SCI075000 SCIENCE / Philosophy & Social Aspects
BISAC: REL106000 RELIGION / Religion & Science

# Contents

Chapter 1 Unbelief and Gen Z ............................................................1

Chapter 2 Does Truth Matter? .......................................................15

Chapter 3 What Else in the Bible is False?.......................................18

Chapter 4 When Did Evolution Become Mainstream? ........................26

Chapter 5 Supernaturalism and Naturalism.....................................59

Chapter 6 Can We Save Our Gen Z Catholics? ...............................65

Chapter 7 Bury the Zombies ........................................................71

Chapter 8 The War for Souls and Cultural Survival ..........................100

Chapter 9 Calling All Catholic Intellectuals ...................................105

Appendix I Is Our Lady's Ancestor a Beast?...................................115

Appendix II Science and Catholicism Resources ............................121

"…almost every Christian heresy can be traced in some form to an attempt to separate God the Creator from God the Redeemer. Christianity stands against that. The gospel of Jesus Christ makes no sense unless you put it in the context of the total story of God's creative and redemptive work, from *Genesis* to *Revelation.*"

Dr Albert Mohler

# Chapter 1
## Unbelief and Gen Z

According to Pew Research, nearly half of U.S. adults under 30 do not believe in Christianity's God and the degree of even a remote affiliation with any Christian religion varies by age group. A Barna Research study released in January 2018, "Atheism Doubles Among Generation Z" (born in/after 1995) reported that

> they are the first truly 'post-Christian' generation. More than any other generation before them, Gen Z does not assert a religious identity. … The percentage of Gen Z that identifies as atheist is *double* that of the U.S. adult population. …Three out of four Boomers are Protestant or Catholic Christians (75%), while just three in five 13- to 18-year-olds say they are some kind of Christian (59%)."

Bishop Robert Barron, the world-famous DVD and YouTube evangelist, is Chairman of the Bishops' Committee on Evangelization and Catechesis. At the U.S. Bishops' Conference meeting in June 2019, he spoke of the massive apostasy of Catholic youth and cited statistics such as "half the kids we baptized and confirmed in the last 30 years are now ex-Catholics or unaffiliated." To put that into perspective, he said that "one out of six millennials in the U.S. is now a former Catholic." He claimed that they simply no longer believe the Church's teachings and called that "the bitter fruit of the dumbing down of our faith" as it has been presented in catechesis and apologetics.

The reality is that many of those once-Catholic children of whom Bishop Barron spoke never had the faith or lost it *before confirmation* because of "the dumbing down of our faith." For example, *Our Sunday Visitor Weekly* published on August 27, 2016, an article titled, "Young people are leaving the faith. Here's why: Many youths and young adults who have left the Church point to their belief that there is a disconnect between science and religion." The article was based on two national studies done by the Center for Applied Research in the Apostolate (CARA). The article said:

> The interviews with youth and young adults who had left the Catholic Faith revealed that the typical age for this decision to leave was made at 13. Nearly two-thirds of those surveyed, 63 percent said they stopped being Catholic between the ages of 10 and 17. Another 23 percent say they left the Faith before the age of 10. Those who leave are just as likely to be male as they are female, and their demographics generally mirror those of all young Catholics their age.

The non-profit Pew Research Center's decades long Religious Landscape Project that has documented the steady decline in the percentage of U.S. adults who self-identify as Catholics has also questioned the Catholics who joined the swelling ranks of the religiously unaffiliated (otherwise known as the "nones") about why they left. Contrary to the popular opinion that people leave because of disagreements with the Church's teaching on "hot button" issues such as contraception, same-sex marriage, clerical sexual abusers, etc. the primary reason is far more basic: they simply don't believe in the existence of God.

Since throughout all of known history every culture has had its god or gods and, as St. Paul affirms, "the existence of God can be known by the things he has made," a suitable beginning for determining what needs to be done would be to question why in 21st century America unbelief in God or even "gods" has become a social phenomenon. One factor may be the uncritical acceptance by Catholic clergy and lay intellectuals of scientific speculations which are actually affirmations of faith (i.e., "dogmas") of the non-theistic religion of Humanism first codified in the *Humanist Manifesto* of 1933. Evolutionary cosmology and evolutionary biology which are the materialist scientific consensus regarding our origins are taught as if they were proven facts to children from their earliest school days.

## A Common Denominator

The one thing that the majority of Catholic youth have in common with their fellow Americans is that they were taught, from the earliest days through high school, the materialistic evolutionary theory of origins as a scientific fact. They were taught that in public schools and in many (if not most) Catholic schools. That teaching is reinforced throughout our culture by science and nature- themed programs produced for the Public Broadcasting System (PBS), History Channel, Smithsonian Channel and all public educational sites such as libraries, natural history museums and National Parks. The net result is that the majority of students understand evolutionary origins to be a proved fact. Consider this college girl's understanding of origins: https://cal-catholic.com/west-valley-college-atheist-explains-her-concept-of-the-universe/

A Catholic reading this who also believes evolution to be a proved fact, may be wondering what this writer's problem is with that. Understandably so, because the majority of American Catholics accept that evolutionary theories of origins are factual. According to a study published in December 2013 by the Pew Research Center,

> Six-in-ten Americans (60%) say that "humans and other living things have evolved over time," while a third (33%) reject the idea of evolution, saying that "humans and other living things have existed in their present form since the beginning of time." The share of the general public that says that humans have evolved over time is about the same as it was in 2009, when Pew Research last asked the question.

The report said that 68% of white, non-Hispanic Catholics believe that humans evolved from animals over time and just 26% believe that humans existed in present form since the beginning. The only groups with a higher belief in human evolution than white, non-Hispanic Catholics are the unaffiliated (76%) and mainline Protestants (78%). Among white Evangelical Christians, 64% believe that humans were created as they are now, just as the Fathers, Doctors, Councils and Popes have taught.

A follow up survey by Pew in 2014 found that belief in evolution continued to trend upward when compared to the results published in 2013:

TABLE 1

| First Question | Second Question | April 2013 | August 2014 |
|---|---|---|---|
| Humans have Evolved | | 60% | 65% |
| | Due entirely to natural process? | 32% | 35% |
| | Supreme Being guided evolution? | 24% | 24% |
| | Evolved but don't know how? | 4% | 5% |
| Humans have existed in present form since beginning | | 33% | 31% |
| Don't Know | | 7% | 4% |

In the data from 2013 and 2014 above, an initial question asked respondents whether they think humans and other living things have evolved over time – in line with Charles Darwin's theory of evolution – or whether they believe humans have existed in their present form since the beginning of time, as in the Book of *Genesis*. Those who said they accept the idea of evolution then were asked a second question: whether they think evolution occurred due to natural processes such as natural selection, or due to processes that were guided or allowed by God.

In 2019 Pew Research experimented to see if the way the question was asked influenced the outcome. Half of the respondents were asked in a two-step process as described above. In the 2019 two-step process, the percentage of Catholics who believe in the special creation of humans was about the same as in the 2014 survey, 29%. The other half were asked just one question but were asked to choose one of three possible replies that were offered to them. The single question was: "Which statement comes closest to your view?" The choices offered and the percentages of those choosing the answer are shown in the table below:

TABLE 2

| Humans have evolved over time due to processes such as natural selection; God or a higher power had no role in this process | Humans have evolved over time due to processes that were guided or allowed by God or a higher power. | Humans have existed in their present form since the beginning of time |
| --- | --- | --- |
| 33% overall | 48% overall | 18% overall but Catholics 13% |

Based on that data, 82% of American adults believe in evolution of humans from some sort of evolving animal. And 87% of Catholic adults believe that.

Pew's report of the 2019 result emphasizes the drop in the percentage of those who answer that "Humans have existed in their present form since the beginning of time." depending on how the question is asked. As shown in Table 1 it was 33% in 2013 and 31% in 2014 for the two-step method. As shown in Table 2, with a single question and three choices to answer, it was 18% by all respondents and 13% by Catholic respondents. These lower numbers of belief according to *Genesis* are probably more reflective of the actual state of belief.

## Theistic Evolution

As noted in Table 2 above, perhaps 48 out of 100 American adults find a "third way" between the scientific consensus and the text of the Bible. While accepting that "something" turned into "everything" over billions of years, as taught to them in school, they overlay it with the belief that some Supreme Being guided evolution. (That would make it a directed undirected process!) The combination of belief in evolution as a proved scientific fact but then overlaid with belief in guidance by God at one or more points in, or prior to, a supposed multi-billion-year process defines the theistic evolution theory of origins. Among theistic evolutionists there is extreme vagueness about what those supernatural interventions were and when they happened. Some Catholics who hold that combination have been taught philosophical proofs for the existence of God and have been told that evolution was the playing out of secondary causes flowing according to Divine Providence from the original "whatever it was" created from nothing "whenever." It "works" for them. Since they have reached mature adulthood and feel their Faith is fully intact, it is practically impossible to convince them that belief in evolution is causing others to lose their Faith. Many Catholics simply "tune out" to objections to evolution, such as the lack of scientific evidence, and other rational arguments such as "truth matters." Others accuse fiat creationists of being an embarrassment to the Church by being so "backward."

Belief in evolution often leads to a situation where Catholics lose respect for Catholics who dissent from Darwinian orthodoxy. Often this antagonism is associated with little understanding of the ideological bias of "evolutionary science," and how the "settled

science" taught in school is so different from the science problems discussed in peer-reviewed professional journals. Relying on the maxim that "there can be no conflict between true science and true religion because God is author of both," many Catholic intellectuals, lay and clerical, sincerely believe that theistic evolution blends faith with scientific credibility. But the school kids are not "buying" it and the refusal to acknowledge that they aren't buying is self-inflicted blindness. Richard Dawkins, world-famous evolutionary biologist and atheist author (*The God Delusion, The Blind Watchmaker*) ridicules theistic evolutionists: "Theistic evolutionists are deluded." Watch this 1-minute video as Dawkins explains why
https://www.youtube.com/watch?v=BAbpfn9QgGA

### The Church Once Taught Creation

The Church, which has the truth about our origins, has ceded the education of its youth on these matters to the secular culture to provide explanations for which no God was necessary. World-famous author, lecturer, and prominent spokesman for "the New Atheists," Richard Dawkins, has explained that Darwinism makes theistic belief both implausible and unnecessary: "Darwin made it possible to be an intellectually fulfilled atheist."

The Catholic Church has the truth about the supernatural origin of the world and its inhabitants but it has yielded the education of its youth on these matters to the civil culture. We have ignored paragraph 282 of the 1994 *Catechism of the Catholic Church.*

> Catechesis on creation is of major importance. It concerns the very foundations of human and Christian life: for it makes explicit the response of the Christian faith to the basic question that men of all times have asked themselves: "Where do we come from?" "Where are we going?" "What is our origin?" "What is our end?" "Where does everything that exists come from and where is it going?" The two questions, the first about

the origin and the second about the end, are inseparable. They are decisive for the meaning and orientation of our life and actions.

Have the teaching institutions of the Church in America (or elsewhere) carried out a catechesis responsive to paragraph 282? Or have they promulgated what Bishop Barron calls the "dumbing-down of our faith?" Cardinal Ratzinger, who became Pope Benedict XVI, published in 1995 a book called *In the Beginning...* In that book's Preface the Cardinal wrote that:

> ...the creation account is noticeably and completely absent from catechesis, preaching, and even theology. The creation narratives go unmentioned; it is asking too much to expect anyone to speak of them.

That lament, on the failure at all levels to convincingly answer the questions identified in paragraph 282, was a problem he had been pointing out to bishops and other educators for years.

In a lecture delivered January 27, 1988, at St. Peter's Church in New York, Cardinal Ratzinger, then-Prefect of the Congregation for the Doctrine of the Faith, explained how Rudolf Bultmann used the assumption that the evolutionary explanation of origins was a naturalistic fact to "demystify" the Bible. Origination of the "scientific method" of interpreting the Bible is credited to German Protestant Bultmann, born in 1884. He became a university professor in 1921, when evolution theories and non-theistic philosophy were already the rule in German universities. The title of Ratzinger's lecture was "Biblical Interpretation in Crisis: On the Question of the Foundations and Approaches of Exegesis Today."

> In the first place, one can note that in the history-of-religions school, the model of evolution was applied to the analysis of biblical texts. This was an effort to bring the methods and models of the natural sciences to bear on the study of history.

Bultmann laid hold of this notion in a more general way and thus attributed to the so-called scientific worldview a kind of dogmatic character. Thus, for example, for him the non-historicity of the miracle stories [in the Bible] was no question whatever anymore. The only thing one needed to do yet was to explain how these miracle stories came about. On one hand the introduction of the scientific worldview was indeterminate and not well thought out. On the other hand, it offered an absolute rule for distinguishing between what could have been and what had to be explained only by development. To this latter category belonged everything which is not met with in common daily experience. There could only have been what now is. For everything else, therefore, historical processes are invented, whose reconstruction became the particular challenge of exegesis…To that extent there lies in modern exegesis a reduction of history into philosophy, a revision of history by means of philosophy.

In a May 1989 address to the Presidents of the European Doctrinal Commissions, speaking then as Prefect of the Congregation for the Doctrine of the Faith, Cardinal Ratzinger's talk was on the "Difficulties Confronting the Faith in Europe Today." He traced through the litany of issues pertaining to sexual morality and the Church's sacramental order, and said they are linked together by the same false vision of humanity. He went on to say that:

> We can give a proper answer to the conflict in detail only if we keep all of the relationships in view. It is their disappearance which has robbed the Faith of its reasonableness. In this context, I would like to list three areas within the worldview of the Faith which have witnessed a certain kind of reduction in the last centuries, a reduction which has been gradually preparing the way for another "paradigm."

*In the first place, we have to point out the almost complete disappearance of the doctrine on creation from theology.* [Emphasis added.] As typical instances, we may cite two compendia of modern theology in which the doctrine on creation is eliminated as part of the content of the faith and is replaced by vague considerations from existential philosophy, [he then named two published in Europe]. In a time when we are experiencing the agonizing of creation against man's work and when the question of the limits and standards of creation upon our activity has become the central problem of our ethical responsibility, this fact must appear quite strange. Notwithstanding all this, it remains always a disagreeable fact that 'nature' should be viewed as a moral issue...That nature has a mathematically intelligibility is to state the obvious, the assertion that it also contains in itself a moral intelligibility, however is rejected as a metaphysical fantasy. The demise of metaphysics goes hand in hand with the displacement of the teaching on creation.

The "another paradigm" of which Ratzinger spoke was ushered in by the methods of Bultmann he had criticized the year before in New York. It would be wrong to think that a German Protestant was the only scholar who had latched on to Darwin's theory published in 1859 and held it as a matter of faith to which the Bible's text had to be reinterpreted. For example, Jesuits George Tyrrell (1861-1909) and Alfred Loisy (1857-1940) were among the early Catholic scholars who, like Bultmann, specialized in the rejection of any idea of supernatural revelation. They ran afoul of the Vatican because of their opinions and they left the priesthood and the Church.

Cardinal Ratzinger's statements detailing the impact that believing evolution was a proved fact has had on biblical interpretation (demystification) and on philosophy and theology also reveals that clergy are not educated and prepared in the seminary to teach the creation doctrines, at least not with rationality and conviction. Arguably, the majority of clergy believe that the theory of cosmic and biological evolution they learned in school is science. The "scientific method" of biblical exegesis based on that theory that is taught in many seminaries helps priests to interpret the Bible in accordance with the secular "creation" account of origins. By so "interpreting," they can believe in evolution while still affirming the dogma that the Bible is inerrant and that even if cosmic and biological evolution are true, "God did it." But what they can't do is teach the Catholic creation doctrines of *Genesis* with which the Bible begins with the knowledge and conviction needed to convince the majority of teens that the supernatural explanation, not the naturalistic explanation, is the correct one. So, the teens leave.

The point is that some teachers undermine belief in *Genesis* (and thus the Bible as a whole) by substituting materialistic hypothesis such as the "big bang" and biological evolution while also trying to "baptize" them by asserting that "God did it."

Some theistic evolutionists posit that all God did was create matter and did not intervene directly after that. Some Christians, such as those at the Biologos Foundation, have long subscribed to that "creation" theory that is akin to Deism. Because the scientific consensus has no plausible theory for the source of matter and energy in the "singularity," that was the source of the "Big Bang," that is where God fits in: He created the singularity.

Some Catholic evolutionists are a little more nuanced in their theories. Some have a convoluted "theological" theory that contravenes the known natural laws and proposes that matter operated contingently but according to "divine causality" and "divine providence" to produce the evolutionary process of creation. That notion surfaced in an 1887 book by a French Dominican, Fr. M. D. Léroy, that was rejected by the Vatican. (Details of that follow in Chapter 4.)

11

"Secondary causality" as the explanation for evolution was resurrected and made its way back into "mainstream" Catholic education as part of a wide-ranging 95-numbered paragraphs document produced circa 2003 by the International Theological Commission (ITC) called "Communion and Stewardship." The ITC consists of 30 theologians appointed by the Pope for 5-year terms to advise the Congregation for the Doctrine of the Faith. Because theistic evolution is mainstream in Catholic theological circles, that particular mish-mash of the secular "scientific consensus" with "advanced" theological thinking found its way into 4 of the paragraphs. Evolutionist promoters of that document, among them the theology chairman at a self-described "orthodox" Catholic college, make much of the fact that Cardinal Ratzinger was *ex-officio* President of the ITC at that time and approved its publication. Nevertheless, it is not part of the authentic Magisterium because it was not in a style or promulgated in a manner that indicated it was for the belief of the universal Church.

### The Substitute for Belief in the God of *Genesis*

G. K. Chesterton wrote that "When men cease to believe in God, they do not then believe in nothing, they believe in anything." What do Catholic youth believe in? The preeminent social researcher on the religious knowledge and attitudes of American youths is Christian Smith, Ph.D., a professor of sociology at the University of Notre Dame. Smith has been tracking and personally interviewing various huge cohorts of U.S. youth for nearly two decades, thanks to a grant from the Eli Lilly Foundation. Smith himself is a convert and in his first book, *Soul Searching*, he devoted a chapter to the fact that of all Christian youth he interviewed it was the Catholics who were least likely to articulate what their Faith was. Smith has asserted that the dominant faith American youngsters hold is what he calls Moralistic Therapeutic Deism (MTD). MTD is "colonizing" Catholicism itself, as this new "pop culture" religion seduces converts who never have to leave their Christian identification as they embrace this new faith and all of its undemanding dimensions. People can even remain affiliated with their parents' religion while believing nothing of it. Read about MTD here. https://scienceandcatholicism.org/mtd/

There is a video on YouTube called "How American Youth (Mis)Understand Science and Religion." In the video, Professor Smith lectures to a room full of bishops and priests at the Symposium on Pastoral Issues in Science and Human Dignity held at Notre Dame in February 2014. He explains to them that of all of the religious denominations in the U.S., it was the young Catholics who were contributing most to the growth of the "nones." ("Nones" are people who never were or are no longer affiliated with a religion.) He explains how easily it is for poorly educated Catholics to be peeled away from the True Faith because of what he calls "faux science." https://www.youtube.com/watch?v=OaS1SV7xwWQ

Other social researchers have found the same weakness and susceptibility to "faux science" in Catholic youth. In the aforementioned two national studies by the Center for Applied Research in the Apostolate (CARA) that showed how many Catholics lose their faith as teens, the studies found they are leaving because of what they see as a disconnect between religion and science. Teenagers want to know where we came from, why we are here, and what the purpose of life is. In school, they are taught a naturalist scientific explanation of origins involving untold ages of things happening by random chance that resulted in the universe and us. No God was necessary. It all happened by cosmic and biological evolution. By the time they are teens, most children of Catholic or Christian parents would have heard some sort of a supernatural explanation involving God, the Bible perhaps, and the vaguely articulated word "creation." This can lead to "cognitive dissonance." "Cognitive dissonance" is defined as a situation involving *conflicting* attitudes, beliefs, or behaviors. This produces a *feeling of discomfort,* leading to an alteration in one of the attitudes, beliefs, or behaviors to reduce the discomfort and restore balance. At some point, teenagers recognize that the naturalistic evolutionary model of origins and the supernatural, *fiat* creation model described in the Bible, which they have heard read at Mass even if they never opened a Bible, can't both be true. They experience cognitive dissonance, and, to relieve the conflict, they must alter their beliefs in one direction or the other. According to the social researchers, too many teens resolve the disconnect between religion and science in favor of science. After all, "science" delivers the goods such as the machines and gadgets that enrich our lives. The fact is, that's engineering based on operational/empirical science; the "science" of cosmic and biological evolution is speculation based on inferences from historical data. The mechanism by which it happened remains unknown and bound in conundrums. It's tooth fairy science. But the institutions of the Church have ceded the education of youth on these matters to the secular culture. Most Catholic adults (including clergy) are not informed on these matters so they can't help the kids discriminate between "faux science" and real science. On a Sunday in October 2019 my pastor from the pulpit lamented that 70% of Catholics do not believe literally in the Real Presence. If they don't believe the Bible's account of creation is true, why should they believe in the Real Presence? Belief in "faux science" concerning the origin and history of the universe is peeling away Catholic youth.

# Chapter 2
# Does Truth Matter?

The materialists and the scientific consensus are not "buying" the theistic evolution theory. They ridicule it by saying that theists invented it as the explanation for the appearance of purposeful design in that which the scientific consensus "knows" happened by chance. If they also believed "God did it," they wouldn't be materialists. But they don't and they are out-evangelizing us.

Defenders of the literal truth of the Bible agree with the New Atheists on one thing: Truth claims need to be taken seriously—which means they must be evaluated as true or false, not merely interpreted as metaphors and symbols. Catholic evolutionists are squeezed between these two opposing adherents of the "put up or shut up" school of interpretation. Catholic evolutionists think both extremes are simplistic; "it's complicated," they say. The New Atheists have shrugged off this dodge, accusing the Catholic apologists of creating a pseudointellectual smokescreen. And the exit in droves from the Church by Catholic youths indicates that the New Atheists are winning the debate.

World-famous "New Atheist" Richard Dawkins is representative of the evolutionists who admit the universe looks designed, but it just happened that way by pure chance. In fact, he wrote a best-selling book to "prove" it. In his *The Blind Watchmaker: Why the Evidence of Evolution Reveals a Universe* he explained:

> Biology is the study of complicated things that give the appearance of having been designed for a purpose.

Dawkins is an evolutionary biologist. He has Doctorates in Philosophy and Science from Oxford, and has been a professor at both UCal Berkley and Oxford. In addition to his academic career, Dawkins has published 14 books promoting atheism on the basis of evolution that collectively have sold 10 million copies, and, as a result, he has a net worth estimated at over $10 million. My town's public library has copies of at least 10 of his books. He travels the world lecturing and debating on behalf of evolution and atheism. On a TV show, Dawkins was interviewed and asked when he became an atheist.

> And was there a particular point or something that you read or an experience you had that sort of said 'Yep, this is it. God doesn't exist'?

Dawkins replied:

> Oh well, by far the most important I suppose was understanding evolution. I think the Evangelical Christians have really got it right, it in a way, in seeing evolution as the enemy, whereas the more, what shall we say, sophisticated theologians who are quite happy to live with evolution, I think they are deluded. I think the Evangelicals have got it right in that there really is a deep incompatibility between evolution and Christianity and I think I realized that at about the age of 16.

That is about the age the CARA social research quoted earlier shows that Catholic youth are losing their faith. The materialistic scientific consensus of evolution as a random chance process, asserted to be the proof of the world's origins, is taught in school as "science" year in and year out. When the CCD teacher, a priest, or even mom and dad just insert God as the real cause, and throw in an ill-defined concept called "creation" on the basis of "religion," the kids aren't "buying"

16

it either. But they don't want to hurt (or anger) their parents by saying so. At least not while living at home. By overlaying God's supernatural role on the naturalist consensus of evolution, some students (and priests) can arrive at what is, for them, both scientific and religious truth. But is it actually true?

The point is that such explanations are not "scientific," for no scientist would hold that theory, and they are not biblical, because they discount the truth of the inerrancy of Scripture. In short, what is very commonly being taught, and believed, by most Catholics is not anything the Church has ever held to be true. They have no basis in Sacred Tradition. In his book, *Aquinas and Evolution,* Dominican priest Michael Chaberek explained why priests and lay intellectuals fall into this error. He wrote that theologians and philosophers don't know natural science well enough to be able to distinguish scientific facts from the materialistic interpretations, and dread being called "anti-scientific." Their exaggerated esteem, or even fear of the "scientific community," makes them unable to question the so-called "scientific consensus," so they have adopted the naturalistic paradigm. In a sense, those priests and lay intellectuals are caught in a scientific "time warp." They are holding onto 19th Century science that has been refuted by 21st Century science but which is still being promoted in cultural institutions because it is integral to the secular Humanist philosophical word view it spawned. These are scientific zombies; dead but unburied and still walking through textbooks and classrooms.

# Chapter 3
## What Else in the Bible is False?

*If Genesis 1-3* is not history and the "scientific" explanation of our origins is to be preferred as long as we throw "God did it" somewhere into the process, what is it exactly? What is the "cost" of the "theistic evolution" approach to the credibility of the Bible as a whole?

The Bible is an integrated document. But theistic evolution as commonly taught denies at least 11 creation events and undermines crucial doctrines. The question is whether *Genesis* 1-3 is a historical narrative in the sense of reporting events that the Author wants readers to believe actually happened (not "figurative" or "allegorical" literature).

Although not all theistic evolutionists believe the points below, these are the logical implications of the evolutionary hypothesis as taught by the scientific consensus:

- All living things have come about not through direct creation by special activity by God, but by random mutation from previous, simpler life forms that evolved from non-living elements such as what the highly-credentialed priest called "primordial slime." (In school they tell the kids life spontaneously arose from "primordial soup.") We have descended from earlier creatures by virtue of random mutations and natural election with or without God guiding it. (This is asserted even though there is no known mechanism by which any of that could have happened naturally.)
- There was no "original couple" from whom all humans descended. Evolution theory posits that the human race descended from a population of earlier creatures. That aspect of the theory is called polygenism. Some theistic evolutionists assert that if there were an Adam and Eve, they were chosen

from the population and so named by God. Granted that most Catholic theistic evolutionists who are "mainstream" and have been taught that belief in a first man from whom the human race descended is a doctrine assert that they do believe it. In paragraph 37 of *Humani Generis* Pope Pius XII made the binding theological statement that is incompatible with the theory of evolution, namely, that all humans are descendent from one man, Adam.

> For the faithful cannot embrace that opinion which maintains that either after Adam there existed on this earth true men who did not take their origin through natural generation from him as from the first parent of all, or that Adam represents a certain number of first parents.

This belief conflicts with the theory of evolution as it is. It requires a miraculous or supernatural intervention of some sort. It is one of those "god-of-the gaps" explanations on which theistic evolutionists rely to keep "one foot in each camp," so to speak. They have no coherent explanation compatible with the theory of evolution. What it really may indicate is the shallowness of their understanding of the implications of a scientific hypothesis they otherwise support as a better explanation of cosmic and biological origins than the Bible. It's very facile for such Catholic evolutionists to pose as "scientific" and "orthodox" but a little more difficult for them to expend the mental energy necessary to become coherent in their belief.

How do the implications of the evolutionary hypothesis impact *Genesis* 1-3? Here are 11 events denied by the evolution theory (as taught by the scientific consensus and properly understood) :

1. Adam and Eve were not the first human beings and may not have existed.
2. Adam and Eve, if they existed, were not created without parents but were born from parents.

3. God did not act directly or specially create Adam out of the dust of the ground.

4. God did not directly create Eve from a rib taken from Adam's side.

5. Adam and Eve did not commit the first human sin (Original Sin) and were probably not completely innocent human beings for there is no reason to believe they were morally different from the population of which they were part.

6. Human death did not begin as a result of Adam's sin because human beings and other creatures existed before Adam and they were subject to death.

7. Not all human beings descended from Adam and Eve because there were other human beings on the Earth if and when God chose them to be known as Adam and Eve.

8. God did not directly act in the natural world to create different "kinds" of fish, birds, and land animals.

9. God did not "rest" from His work of creation or stop any special creative activity after plants, animals and human beings appeared on the Earth.

10. God never created an originally "very good" natural world in the sense of a world that was a safe environment free of thorns and thistles and similar harmful things.

11. After Adam and Eve sinned, God did not place any curse on the world that changed the workings of the natural world and made it more hostile to mankind.

It seems that theistic evolution sees *Genesis 1-3* as figurative or allegorical literature, not as factual history. Is there an argument from the Bible itself that *Genesis 1-3* is factual history? In brief, here are some reasons:

1. *Genesis 1-3* has a narrative structure. There is a variety of literary forms in the Bible. Many biblical texts describe creation events in poetic form. For example, on Trinity Sunday in 2019 the First Reading (Proverbs 8:22-31) and the

Responsorial Psalm (Psalm 8: 4-9) describe creation events in poetic style.

> When I behold your heavens, the work of your fingers/
> The moon and the stars which you have set in place-
> What is man that you should be mindful of him/

But the historical narratives found throughout the Bible have a certain structure and no translation changed it to something like a poetic form.

2. Its placement as the first chapters in the first book is significant. The whole Bible has a chronological sequence from revealing where we came from in *Genesis* to *Revelation*, the last book, which reveals the ending.

3. *Genesis* 1-3 has many inter-textual ties to later Old Testament narratives. For example, *Genesis* 5:3-6 narrates that, "When Adam had lived 130 years he fathered a son … and named him Seth. After Seth was born, Adam lived 800 years and had other sons and daughters. … When Seth had lived 105 years, he became the father of Enosh." That genealogy continues in *Genesis* up to Abraham whose father was Terah who descended from Shem whose father was Noah (*Genesis* 11: 10-26.) Abraham, Isaac, and Jacob were certainly historical figures.

4. There is a good argument for historicity based on the macro-structure of *Genesis*. The phrase "this is the generations of," "these are the descendants of," or similar is used 11 times.

> *Gen* 2:4 "These are the generations of the heavens and the earth when they were created."
> *Gen* 5:1 "This is the list of the descendants of Adam."
> *Gen* 6:9 "These are the descendants of Noah."
> *Gen* 10:1 "These are the descendants of Noah's sons, Shem, Ham, and Japheth"
> *Gen* 11:10 "These are the descendants of Shem."

*Gen* 11:27 "Now these are the descendants of Terah."[Father of Abraham]

*Gen* 25:19 "These are the descendants of Isaac, Abraham's son:"

*Gen*: 38:2 "This is the story of the family of Jacob."

Note: In the New Testament this structure continues.

*Matthew* 1:1 "An account of the genealogy of Jesus the Messiah, the son of David, the son of Abraham."

In all of these the writer is giving a narrative clearly intended as history.

5.  Ten New Testament books reaffirm the historicity of specific details in *Genesis* 1-3:

- *Matthew* 19: 4-5 [Jesus quoting *Genesis 1:27* and *Genesis 2:24*] "He who created them from the beginning made them male and female, and said, 'Therefore a man shall leave his father and his mother and hold fast to his wife, and the two shall become one flesh.'" The "therefore" in the quote from Gen 2:24 refers to the creation of Eve from Adam's rib.

- *Luke* 3:38 [Luke's genealogy of Jesus] "the son of Enos, the son of Seth, the son of Adam, the son of God."

- *Acts* 17:24 "The God who made the world and everything in it." *Acts* 17:26 "And he made from one man every nation of mankind to live on all the face of the Earth."

- *Romans* 5:12-19 "Therefore, just as sin came into the world through one man, and death came through sin, … For if the many died through the one man's trespass, … For just as by the one man's disobedience the many were made sinners, so by the one man's obedience the many will be made righteous."

- *1 Corinthians* 11:8 "For man was not made from woman, but woman from man." *1 Cor* 15:21-22 "For as by a man came death, by a man has come also the resurrection of the dead. For as in Adam all die, so also in Christ shall all be made alive." 1 Cor 15:45 "Thus it is written, 'the first man Adam became a living being;' the last Adam became a life-giving spirit." *1 Cor* 15:47 "The first man was from the earth, a man of dust…"
- *2 Corinthians* 11:3 "But I am afraid as the serpent deceived Eve by his cunning, your thought will be led astray from a sincere and pure devotion to Christ."
- *Colossians* 1:16 "For by him all things were created, in heaven and on earth, visible and invisible."
- *1 Timothy* 2:13 "For Adam was formed first, then Eve." *1 Tim* 2:14 "and Adam was not deceived, but the woman was deceived and became a transgressor."
- *Hebrews* 4: 4-10 "For he has somewhere spoken of the seventh day in this way 'And God rested on the seventh day from all his works.'… For whoever has entered God's rest has also rested from his works as God did from his."
- *Revelation* 4:11 "Worthy are you, our Lord and God, to receive glory and honor and power, for you created all things, and by your will they existed and were created." *Rev* 10:6 "… him who lives forever and ever, who created heaven and what is in it, the earth and what is in it, and the sea and what is in it."

To accept theistic evolution coherently one has to accept that 10 books of the New Testament are wrong in treating *Genesis* 1-3 as historical narrative. These books are regularly read from at Mass, either as one of the Readings or as the Gospel. When the lector finishes the Reading at Mass with "The Word of the Lord," the people respond "Thanks be to God." When the Gospel has been read, the reader says "The Gospel of the Lord" and the people respond with "Praise to You Lord Jesus Christ." Perhaps that has become robotic but literally it is an assent to one's belief that the reading from some part of the Bible just completed is in fact what the authoritative teaching of the Church says it is, namely, the inerrant words written by the human instruments of the Divine Author. Theistic evolutionists in the congregation are simultaneously affirming and denying inerrancy when anything is read from one of those 10 books.

Fundamental doctrines are undermined by theistic evolution and here are just three:

1.  The inerrancy of the Bible is a doctrine upheld recently in *Dei Verbum* ("Dogmatic Constitution on Divine Revelation") that was published in 1965 as one of the documents of the Second Vatican Council. That teaching was included in the 1994 *Catechism of the Catholic Church* (paragraph 107). Proponents of evolution essentially claim that there are whole areas of human knowledge of which the Bible speaks without authority. They refer to the "conditional inerrancy" of the Bible.

2.  That the existence of God can be known by the things He has made is a doctrine. Its scriptural basis is *Romans* 1:18-20 "For the wrath of God is revealed from heaven against all ungodliness and wickedness of men who by their wickedness suppress the truth. For what can be known about God is plain to them, because God has shown it to them. Ever since the creation of the world his invisible nature, namely, his eternal power and deity, has been clearly perceived in the things that have been made. So they are without excuse;" Promotion of evolution has provided an excuse in a way. If a person is indoctrinated from childhood with stories of cosmic and biological evolution by the authority figures over him, perhaps he can be in "invincible ignorance" on this matter.

3. Our moral accountability to God which is summarized in *Acts* 17 and based on creation is undermined by theistic evolution. Paul told the men of Athens:

> The God who made the world and everything in it, being Lord of heaven and earth, does not live in shrines made by man, ... And he made from one every nation of men to live on all the face of the earth, having determined allotted periods and the boundaries of their habitation, ... The times of ignorance God overlooked, but now he commands all men everywhere to repent, because he has fixed a day on which he will judge the world in righteousness by a man whom he has appointed, and of this he has given assurance to all men by raising him from the dead.

# Chapter 4
# When Did Evolution
# Become Mainstream?

It wasn't always "mainstream" within Catholic intellectual circles to interpret our origins as an eon-long progressive "creation" micromanaged by God. When naturalism, fueled by the appearance of Darwin's books, *The Origin of Species...* (1859) and *The Decent of Man... (1871)* got into high gear toward the end of the 19th Century it was strongly refuted by the Church's Magisterium. An account of the Church's early response to Darwinism was made possible in recent decades when the Congregation for the Doctrine of the Faith made its archives up to the end of 1903 available to researchers. "Early Vatican Responses to Evolutionist Theology" is an article based on research in those archives by Fr. Brian Harrison and published by the Roman Theological Forum in May 2001. An internet search for that paper finds it but when one clicks on the url given for it the article doesn't come up and it looks like some other organization has usurped the site. That research is so important that it must not be lost to the public. Therefore, the majority of Fr. Harrison's article is reprinted below in this chapter. One thing to keep in mind while reading this is that while evolution's status has reached cultural ascendancy in current times, the 19th Century science upon which it is based has largely been refuted by 21st Century science. If that is "news" to you, you can find the proof in my book, *Creation, Evolution, and Catholicism: A Discussion for Those Who Believe.*

## Early Vatican Responses to Evolutionist Theology
## By Brian W. Harrison

Shortly after Darwin's *Origin of Species* appeared in 1859, the first significant magisterial response on the part of the Successors of the Apostles was that of the German Catholic bishops, who, in their

Provincial Council of Cologne (1860), condemned the idea of natural human evolution in no uncertain terms:

> Our first parents were formed immediately by God. Therefore we declare that the opinion of those who do not fear to assert that this human being, man as regards his body, emerged finally from the spontaneous continuous change of imperfect nature to the more perfect, is clearly opposed to Sacred Scripture and to the Faith.[1]

In the next decades, no declarations were made on this subject by the Holy See, although Vatican Council I had on its agenda a reaffirmation of God's special creation of the bodies of Adam and Eve, and probably would have promulgated this teaching had the Council not been cut short by the Franco-Prussian war. Nevertheless, Rome's silence in response to Germany's eloquence obviously signified her consent, since those bishops were simply repeating what the Church had always taught, and what was taught in all approved Catholic theology faculties at the time.

The hypothesis of human evolution attracted renewed attention in the Vatican when a letter dated June 20, 1894, from a French layman, M. Charles Chalmel, arrived at the Holy Office, submitting two questions, the first of which is prefaced by the following remarks, reproduced in the *Acta* of the Congregation:

> A Dominican scholar, Fr. Léroy, a friend of Fr. Monsabré (who shares his opinions), has published a book, *L'évolution restreinte aux espèces organiques, par le père Léroy dominicain.* Now, in this work upholding the opinion of Darwin, the author affirms that in the Genesis narrative the only truths of orthodoxy are "the creation of the universe by God and the action of His providence; that the 'how' of creation is left to human investigation; that Moses' narrative is 'an old patriarchal song, . . . a tissue of metaphors', and that science cannot take any account of the literal sense of Genesis".[2] [That is pretty much what some theistic evolutionists hold in 2020]

M. Chalmel's first question is whether the Holy Office approved of this new interpretation of *Genesis*. His second question, curiously, is whether it is true that the 1632 [*sic*] Decree of the Holy Office against Galileo has been annulled.[3] It was probably inevitable that the specter of the Galileo case should rise once again in this context, now that the most important challenge to faith from the physical sciences in more than two and a half centuries was forcing itself upon the attention of Church authority.

The record of a Holy Office meeting three months later (September 19, 1894) notes that Fr. M. D. Léroy's book has been evaluated by a consultor for the Congregation, Fr. Domenichelli.[4] Perhaps surprisingly, this theologian concluded that the accused author's novel views arrived at, but did not transgress, the limit of what Catholic orthodoxy could accommodate. Domenichelli's appeal for tolerance toward Léroy includes the observation that the book appeared seven years earlier (in 1887): meanwhile, it has been "running round the world unimpeded; and the Church has so far remained silent". Indeed, the Holy Office consultor adds, similar *de facto* freedom has been accorded to other books still more daring than that of Fr. Léroy.[5]

But while, as a consequence of Fr. Domenichelli's positive evaluation, the meeting that day refrained from placing Léroy's work on the Index of Forbidden Books,[6] the matter was by no means considered settled. The details of what transpired in the next few months are not recorded in the *Acta* of the Holy Office, but the Congregation's authorities evidently wanted several other opinions before coming to a decision. As matters turned out, all three of these new consultors, whose opinions were recorded at the Congregation's next meeting on January 21, 1895, expressed their decided opposition to Fr. Léroy's evolutionist theology of human origins. One of them, Fr. E. Buonpensiere, O.P., was bluntly dismissive of his French Dominican confrère's approach:

> Fr. Léroy, . . . instead of combating the absurd opinion of evolutionist anthropologists with the dictates of Revelation, seeks to harmonize evolution with Sacred Scripture and Divine Tradition. . . Evolution, as all Catholic philosophers

teach, stands resolutely condemned by the science of ontology as well as by empirical science.[7]

The former science, Buonpensiere explains, demonstrates that essences are unchangeable, while the latter shows that hybrids are sterile. "This providential law regarding hybrids," he asserts, "breaks through the ranks of all the evolutionist sophistries".[8] Léroy's views, therefore, are roundly condemned as "anti-Christian and anti-Catholic". Buonpensiere draws on St. Thomas' teaching in *ST* Ia, Q. 91, a. 2, and Q. 92, a. 4, to the effect that Adam's body could not have come about through any created power. He concludes that Léroy's book should thus be either proscribed (placed on the Index) or suppressed.[9] Another consultor, Bishop E. Fontana of Cremona, was equally unimpressed by Léroy: "I express the desire that the author be seriously warned and repressed in the intemperance and audacity of his thoughts, which will please evolutionists as well as atheists and materialists, but which cannot be accepted by true Catholics."[10]

By far the most substantial critique of Léroy, however, came from the Holy Office's third new consultor, Fr. Luigi Tripepi, whose 54-page booklet, dated December 8, 1894, was also placed on the table at the Holy Office meeting six weeks later.[11] Since the commentaries of Domenichelli and Tripepi contain the substantial briefs presented to the Holy Office judges for the 'defense' and 'prosecution' of Léroy's thesis, it will be useful to summarize here the principal points of their respective cases.

### The Defense: Fr. Domenichelli

Right from the beginning, Fr. Domenichelli's argument signals the fact that he, as much as Léroy, is very conscious of the huge historic embarrassment for the Church that was occasioned by the Galileo case and its aftermath in subsequent centuries. He notes that the French theologian

> hopes that the theory of evolution will have the same destiny as that of the Copernican or Galilean theory: he hopes, that is, that after having aroused the ire of believers, it will, after

the dust has settled, be purified of every exaggeration on the one hand, and on the other hand, end in triumph.[12]

The desire to avoid another monumental conflict (or perceived conflict) between science and theology will, it would seem, be a key element in Domenichelli's approach to evolution. He continues by noting (with implied approval) several of Léroy's contentions: that the Church has so far condemned only atheistic evolution; that the Bible tells us nothing of the *manner* in which plants and animals were made; and that evolution is not contrary to Tradition, insofar as Augustine, with his idea of *rationes seminales*, comes quite close to evolution.[13]

In support of the view that the Church has not insisted on a literal interpretation of the early chapters of Genesis, Domenichelli goes on to appeal to the authority of St. Thomas Aquinas, who expresses the opinion (in II Sent., dist. XII, 9, a. 11) that "Moses, instructing an unlettered people about the creation of the world, divides into parts those things that were really made simultaneously". Acknowledging that Ambrose and other authorities take the Genesis narrative more literally,[14] Domenichelli calls to witness other Fathers whose writings on Genesis he thinks leave room for an evolutionary reading: Clement of Alexandria (*Stromata*, Book VI); Origen (*De princ.*, Book 3, ch. 5); Athanasius (*Opus sex dierum*, Book I); Isidore (*De Summo Bono*, I, 8); Augustine (*De Gen. ad litteram*, IV, 52); Cassiodorus (*Div. Inst.*, 1); Julius Africanus (*Liber super Gen.*); Hugh of St. Victor (*De sacr. Christ. fid.*, I, 1); Chrysostom (*Hom. X in cap. Gen. II*); and many of the later scholastics.[15]

Domenichelli quotes a Franciscan theologian, P. Chrisman (*De mundo*, ch. II) who supports the "day-age" theory for the understanding of *yom* in Genesis 1, but admits that the literal interpretation is more common. He then concludes that, as regards *Genesis* 1, "One may hold, as a legitimate opinion in the Church, that in the *Genesis* cosmogony we find a metaphorical language wherein, as far the history of creation is concerned, there is no dogmatic content other than the fact of creation itself, in time and from nothing."[16] Domenichelli accepts unquestioningly the long geological time-scale of "thousands of centuries", insisting, "Today,

I repeat, any literal explanation of [*Genesis* 1] has become an absurdity". He sweepingly asserts the "absolute impossibility" of "concordist" exegesis — that is, trying to establish a "concord" or harmony between modern science and a literal reading of the *Genesis* hexameron.[17] According to Domenichelli, a theologian as great as Cardinal Newman "showed himself well-disposed" to the new evolutionary theories,[18] while many other respected Catholic authorities such as Msgr. d'Hulst and Msgr. Freppel claim that the immediate creation of the soul by God is the only *de fide* truth in regard to human origins.[19]

The weight of Catholic tradition, however, had insisted on a special intervention of God in the creation of Adam's body, not just his soul. Here an ambiguity appears in Léroy's position. He seems at first to be professing agreement with that tradition. But is his agreement more nominal than real? Domenichelli first quotes a more traditional-sounding passage from Léroy as follows: "Could we not sunder man in twain, attributing the higher part to the immediate action of God and allowing the lower part to be derived from animality? I reply immediately and without hesitation: No."[20] Domenichelli notes that Léroy professes assent to the 1860 declaration by the German bishops at Cologne which we have cited above (and which Domenichelli says was "approved by Rome"): the French scholar finds "the poison" in the condemned proposition precisely in the words *spontanea . . . immutatione* ("spontaneous change"). A "spontaneous" change would be an exclusively *natural* process terminating in a human body, and Léroy denies the possibility of this, pointing out that no body is a *human* body except when informed by a human soul.[21]

In short, Léroy seems to be employing the theological distinction which has come to be known as that between "natural transformism" (condemned by Cologne) and "special transformism", an arguably orthodox version of evolutionary theory. According to the latter hypothesis, the kind of purely natural evolution postulated by Darwin could have taken place up to the hominid stage, but then a special divine intervention in a hominid body (or genetic material) would have been necessary for the production of a truly human body. Domenichelli and Léroy are agreed that "it is impossible, once

31

we admit the divine origin of the soul, to allow that the human body, precisely as human, derives from animality".[22]

However, the distinction between natural and special transformism seems to be blurred by Léroy, insofar as he theorizes that God did not intervene by acting directly and immediately upon the matter He was using *independently of* His infusion of a rational soul (as *Genesis* 2: 7 strongly suggests He did). Rather, according to Léroy, the human body was produced, *as such*, precisely *by* the one divine act of infusing a spiritual soul into what was until that moment non-human. Domenichelli quotes him as affirming: "It is by his in-breathing [of the soul] that the Creator has transformed clay into human flesh".[23] On this account, the change from a non-human creature to the first human body would have been a purely metaphysical, not a physical, one — analogous to the change which takes place in the reverse direction at the moment of every human death: the body then ceases instantly to be a human body *metaphysically* speaking, even though all the *physical* characteristics of the corpse are still human, in the sense that they do not pertain to any other sub-human species.

Domenichelli admits he finds this aspect of Léroy's theory problematical, insofar as it postulates "a natural evolution preparing clay or dust which is destined to become a human body by the infusion of a soul." He goes on: "The human organism could never have been the terminus of a natural evolution. ... Rightly, therefore did the Council of Cologne — cited by Fr. Léroy — condemn that opinion, which Scheeben (*Dogmatica*, Bk. III, n. 384) goes so far as to qualify as heretical"[24]. Domenichelli also quotes another theologian, Riccardo, who likewise holds that it would be contrary to *Gen.* 2: 7, and therefore heretical, to postulate any natural cause by which a material body could become "sufficiently disposed to receive an intellective soul".[25] In short, Domenichelli seems concerned that Léroy, while professing agreement with the Council of Cologne, is in effect only paying it lip-service, insofar as his theory postulates that natural, sub-human causes alone could produce an organism which would be *apt* or *ready* for the infusion of a spiritual, intellectual soul. In that case, this organism would already possess all the *physical* attributes of a true human being.

32

Domenichelli also admits, in regard to the statement in *Gen.* 2: 7 that God "formed man from the dust of the earth", that "an almost unanimous consensus of the Fathers, Doctors and Theologians has understood that phrase literally, and so as to exclude the cooperation of created forces". [26] It is true, he adds, that one also finds a strong contingent of authorities interpreting chapter 1[of Genesis] literally, "but here [i.e., in ch. 2], the consensus is much more complete, and is not broken by energetic and authoritative protests, as occurs in the case of ch. 1; on the contrary, here we have protests in favor of the literal interpretation."[27]

Nevertheless, Domenichelli notes that Aquinas, while teaching the "immediate" creation of Adam's body by God, does not understand that concept in such a way as to exclude necessarily all active participation of creatures in the process; for he says (*ST* Ia, Q. 91, a.2 ad 1) that God could possibly have used angels for "some sort of ministry in the formation of the first human body".[28] This prompts Domenichelli to speculate that this kind of "ministry" might also have been carried by an animal: "Once the angelic ministry is admitted, it seems we should not necessarily reject an animal ministry".[29]

Domenichelli's 26-page evaluation of Léroy's work (accompanying the minutes of the meeting) comes to the following conclusion: "It seems to me . . . that [arguing for] the evolution of an organism which God would then render human touches those limits beyond which boldness would turn into rashness, and so merit condemnation".[30] He therefore recommends that Léroy's book not be censured. Nevertheless, one is left wondering whether this benign conclusion is altogether compatible with the reservations Domenichelli has already expressed. As we have seen, he has quoted with approval other theologians who consider it heretical to maintain that natural causes alone could produce a human body, in the sense of a body *already* disposed or apt to receive a spiritual soul. But this is precisely what Léroy seems to be maintaining. We have seen that his conservative-sounding affirmation that natural, evolutionary causes would be insufficient to produce a "human" body depends on his giving a purely *metaphysical* understanding to the word "human". From an *empirical, biological* standpoint, the

33

organic material into which God first infused a spiritual soul would, according to the logic of Léroy's evolutionary hypothesis, have been already fully human, and so requiring by its very nature the spiritual soul which God then 'breathed' into it. Perhaps it was this uncertainty or ambiguity as to whether "human", in this context, is to be understood physically or only metaphysically, that persuaded Domenichelli to give Léroy the benefit of the doubt, instead of recommending the condemnation of his book.

## The Prosecution: Fr. Tripepi

It may well have been this ambivalence in Fr. Domenichelli's evaluation of the book that persuaded the Holy Office officials to seek three further opinions before coming to a decision. As we have noted, all these other submissions decided against Léroy, and the most substantial of them was that of Fr. Luigi Tripepi, who lost no time in coming to grips directly with the crucial question, which he poses as follows:

> Could one ever explain [the origin of man's body] by a transformation through natural processes and forces, . . . that is, by the natural evolution of an animal organism which reaches the point of requiring the infusion of a human soul — an infusion which results in the organism then becoming, truly and perfectly, a human body? Or rather, must it be admitted that the formation of the first man's body, prior to God's infusion of the soul, came about through the unique and immediate action of God, and that only thus can it be explained?[31]

Léroy, as we have seen, has answered affirmatively to the first question. Tripepi responds first of all that from a scientific standpoint, Léroy's opinion is untenable because there are no facts that support evolution. Anticipating arguments that have surfaced again very forcefully a century later in regard to the total inadequacy of 'chance mutations' as the supposed driving mechanism behind evolution, Tripepi asserts that evolutionists "postulate means for [bringing about] such transformations that are totally insufficient and often ridiculous".[32] He notes that the non-Catholic Professor

Virchow of the University of Berlin has recently abandoned belief in evolution because of the absence of intermediary forms — 'missing links' — in the fossil record.[33] (Once again, this objection sounds a very 'modern' note.) Moreover, Tripepi asks, if Adam's body evolved, why should that have only happened once? Why should we not have to go further and accept polygenism? Indeed, he points out, the scientific advocates of evolution will see Léroy's theory as illogical in reserving a space for the supernatural infusion of a rational soul in man: if lower beings derive their whole nature from lower forms, why should man be an exception? They will insist that a consistent evolutionary approach will require the materialistic view that the soul too evolved.[34]

Tripepi then turns from scientific to theological objections. Can human evolution be reconciled with revelation? He notes that theologians recognize that Adam's body was not created 'immediately', in the sense of directly from nothing, they do teach that it was formed 'immediately' by God 'from the clay of the earth', and that the woman's body was formed from his side. Thus, Catholic theologians,

> on the basis of the authority of Sacred Scripture, understood according to the unanimous interpretation of the holy Fathers, respond with one voice that man's body was formed by the direct and immediate action of God, distinct not only from the first creation of matter, but also from the concurrence which God, as first Cause, gives to the operation of secondary causes".[35]

All of the Fathers, says Fr. Tripepi, distinguish a three-fold action of God in the creation of man: (1) His creation of matter; (2) His formation of the body; and (3) His infusion of the soul. In this, they distinguish the formation of man from that of other creatures.[36] As regards the appeal made by evolutionist theologians to Augustine's well-known *rationes seminales*, Tripepi responds that the great doctor has in mind — at least as regards human origins — a merely *obediential potency* in primitive matter, and so insists that an immediate divine action was required in order to actualize that potency.[37] That clearly has nothing in common with the modern

35

evolutionary hypothesis regarding human origins. As regards Aquinas' position on this issue, Tripepi cites his judgement in *ST* Ia, Q. 91, a. 2 to the effect that "The first formation of the human body could not have been accomplished by any created power, but immediately by God".[38] What of that "ministry of angels", admitted as a possibility by Aquinas, to which Fr. Domenichelli appealed, as we have seen, as a basis for admitting the hypothesis of animal "ministers" in the formation of Adam? Fr. Tripepi points out that the Fathers commonly deny that any angelic ministry was used here. St Thomas indeed allows this as a possibility, but "he does not speak of any angelic ministry in the formation of the human organism itself, that is, in the organization and suitable disposition of that human material, but rather, of a local aggregation of the clay from which God formed the man's body".[39] This, Tripepi adds, is how Suarez explains St. Thomas (in *De oper. sex dierum* 1. 3. c.1, n. 15).

In short, the Holy Office consultor continues, all theologians until recently have taught that God is the *unique efficient cause* of the bodies of our first parents. Now, indeed, Léroy and several other Catholics such as Fabre, Gmeiner, Mivart[40] and Zahm are saying the opposite. However:

> . . . these few cannot diminish in any way the concord among theologians which until recently was full, solemn, uninterrupted and universal, in regard to this question. . . . [They] cannot carry weight in comparison with those in Rome who have carried out serious studies of the Fathers and of the great philosophers and theologians of the Church down through the centuries. Much less can they claim any authority in the face of the elevated wisdom of the Most Eminent Judges of the Roman Congregations".[41]

As regards the theological note to be ascribed to the traditional belief he is defending, Tripepi quotes Cardinal Camillo Mazzella (who had been a professor in Leo XIII's Roman Seminary) to the effect that a doctrine can be *de fide divina* although not yet *de fide catholica* when it is clearly contained in Scripture, but has not so far been authentically proposed as such by the Church, to be believed by all.[42] Tripepi clearly thinks that the immediate formation of

Adam's and Eve's bodies by God falls into this category. He notes that Suarez (*loc. cit.,* nos. 4 and 6) classifies this truth as "Catholic doctrine"; Perrone (*De Deo Creatore*, part 3, ch. 1, p.1) holds that it "pertains to the faith"; while Riccardo holds that the contrary opinion is heretical, insofar as it is opposed to *Genesis*. In any case, Tripepi adds, errors less grave than heresy cannot be embraced by the faithful: "Certainly, it is impossible to regard as safe (*sicura*) a proposition which is opposed to the unanimous consensus of the Fathers and Doctors". [43]

Having thus appealed to the authority of Tradition, Tripepi goes on to add some exegetical comments of his own. The natural sense of Scripture, he insists, must be respected. *Gen.* 1: 26-27 does not mention any intermediary between God and the first man and woman; "indeed, such mediation is excluded; for He alone created the man whom he created in His own image and likeness".[44] In *Gen.* 2: 7, Fr. Tripepi continues, there are clearly two actions of God specified:

> . . . that is, He disposed the already-created clay of the earth in a form which was apt, or required, to be informed by the soul; then He "breathed in his face the breath of life". Moreover, it is said that only *after* the infusion of the soul did the body molded from clay possess life: ". . . and man became a living soul". Thus, prior to that it had no life at all. Therefore, it could not have come about through evolution from any animal.[45]

Tripepi also notes other Old Testament texts which speak of man's formation by God from the earth without a hint of any intermediary: Job 10: 8-9; 33: 4, 6; Sirach 17: 1, and Wisdom 7: 1.[46] Significantly, he appeals to the "undisputed" immediate creation of Eve, which even Léroy admits cannot be given an evolutionary reading: this fact, he comments, "necessarily sheds new light on the formation of Adam as well".[47] (Tripepi's implication seems to be that it would be improbable that only the woman, and not the man as well, should be formed by the direct action of God.)

In response to the warning that the Church must learn from its sorry experience in the Galileo case, and so not risk being proved wrong by modern science, Tripepi replies that there is no significant parallel between that case and the question of evolution, because Galileo's opinion had some support from earlier Fathers, Doctors, Popes and theologians, while this is not true in regard to Léroy's evolutionist hypothesis of human origins.[48] Tripepi also points out that the Congregation for the Index already prohibited back in 1878 another book sustaining precisely the same thesis as Léroy: this book, *De' nuovi studi della Filosofia, Discorsi* by the Italian priest Caverni, was censured on the basis of an opinion written by Cardinal Zigliara.[49] Indeed, Tripepi is clearly anxious for a *public* declaration against human evolution on the part of the Apostolic See. He refers to several other contemporary theologians who are sharply critical of Catholic evolutionists such as Léroy and Mivart, but who are waiting, he says, for *the Church* to pass judgment against such innovators. According to Tripepi, as long as the Roman Magisterium itself appears to be patient or benign towards these evolutionist novelties, the traditional theologians feel that they too should stop short of roundly condemning them. Nevertheless, he notes that not even the innovators are daring to suggest that Eve's body, as well as Adam's, was a product of evolution.[50]

Having dealt with the principal bone of contention in Léroy's book — the alleged evolution of Adam — Tripepi spends a long section of his pamphlet (pp. 31-44) criticizing the French Dominican for accepting and teaching the evolution of lower species as well. He offers exegetical, patristic, and scientific argumentation in favor of the special creation of all 'kinds' by God, and concludes that evolutionary biology as such is not "in harmony with *Genesis*, taken in its most natural sense, nor with the morally unanimous judgment regarding itself which has been given to us by the Fathers and Doctors. Moreover, it is not supported by scientific evidence."[51] [That evidence has not been provided in the more than 100 years since Tripepi made that observation] Fr. Tripepi's only concession to conventional scientific wisdom is his admission that *yom* — "day", in *Genesis* 1 — might possibly mean "an epoch, or indeterminate period of time, since that is an opinion sustained by some Fathers, some Doctors, and some theologians".[52]

In his peroration Tripepi appeals also to the *sensus fidelium* (which Cardinal John Henry Newman famously emphasised in his landmark essay, "On Consulting the Faithful in Matters of Doctrine"): ordinary devout Catholics, Tripepi points out, are scandalized and incredulous at the notion that the human race is descended from ape-like ancestors; and this datum, he says, needs to be taken into account as one witness among others to the faith that has been handed down over the ages.[53] He denounces the cowardice of too many contemporary Catholic scholars, who, by their excessive fear of what "science" has to say, manifest nothing but the weakness of their own faith.[54] [Equally true of Catholic scholars in 2019] Nevertheless, Fr. Tripepi's final recommendation is that Fr. Léroy should be treated with personal gentleness by the Holy Office, taking into his account his known piety, reputation, respectful attitude and good intentions.[55]

This recommendation was in fact followed by the Holy Office, whose Cardinals obviously found Tripepi's 'case for the prosecution' more persuasive that Domenichelli's somewhat hesitant defense of Fr. Léroy. The latter was called to Rome shortly after the January 1895 meeting of the Congregation, was advised that the doctrine expressed in his book was unacceptable, and was instructed to retract it and withdraw his book from circulation. It was then placed on the Index of Forbidden Books.[56] Léroy obeyed with admirable docility and the *Acta* includes a cutting from the leading French newspaper *Le Monde* of March 4, 1895, publishing the Dominican priest's own retraction, dated February 26. The relevant passage reads as follows: "I have learned today that my thesis, which has been examined here in Rome by the competent authority, has been judged unacceptable, above all in what concerns the human body, since it is incompatible with both the texts of Sacred Scripture and the principles of sound philosophy".

It can be noted as a 'postscript' that, several years later, a similar censure was imposed by the Holy Office against the book *Evolution and Dogma*, by J. A. Zahm, who argued along the same lines as Léroy. Zahm, an American professor at Notre Dame University, wrote a letter to the translator of the book dated May 31, 1899 (later published in *Fortnightly Review,* January 1900, p. 37), stating: "I have learned from unquestionable authority that the Holy See is adverse to the further distribution of *Evolution and Dogma*, and I therefore beg you to use all your influence to have the work withdrawn from sale".[57] [ His letter notwithstanding, Fr. Zahm's book and theology remained a fixture in Notre Dame's teaching by a faculty that accepted Darwinism as a proved fact. The book is still available from that giant online book seller.]

What specific conclusions can now be drawn from this study of some important Holy Office archives concerning the relation of evolutionary hypotheses to the Catholic faith?

**1.Regarding human evolution.** In the first place, we are in a position to correct a widespread popular perception about the history of the Church's relations with science. It is commonly held that while the Vatican notoriously blundered in the seventeenth century by condemning Galileo and proscribing all works propagating the Copernican worldview, Rome 'learned her lesson' from having 'burnt her fingers' during that first great outburst of tension between traditional faith and modern scientific theories, and therefore 'prudently' abstained from intervening with similar condemnations the next time around, when evolution became the new bone of contention, even though many theologians were shrilly calling for Darwin's head on a plate. Indeed, it is not uncommon to hear statements to the effect that the Catholic Church "has never had a problem with evolution".

In fact, the record shows great similarities between the initial Vatican responses in both historic controversies. As Galileo was called in and rebuked by the Holy Office, so were Fr. Caverni and Fr. Léroy. As, in the seventeenth century, works defending the Copernican system were placed on the Index of Forbidden Books, so, in the nineteenth, were works defending human evolution — by Caverni, Mivart, Léroy (and possibly others). The main difference seems to have been that, for whatever reason, these anti-Darwinian censures emanating from Rome never received nearly as much publicity as the Galileo case.

There was in fact a consistent, if relatively quiet, rejection of human evolution on the part of the See of Peter throughout the last three decades of the nineteenth century. Apart from the censures just mentioned, the Holy Office consultors Domenichelli and Tripepi both affirm that the anti-Darwinian decision of the German bishops at Cologne in 1860 was "approved" by Rome, and presumably this was the case (although this approval was apparently given little publicity and its documentation may well be still awaiting rediscovery in other archives of the Congregation). By the 1870s, Father (later Cardinal) Mazzella was teaching at the papal seminary in Rome: hence, the fact that his dogmatic theology text, which went through four editions before the end of the century, declares the immediate formation of Adam's body by God to be a "most certain truth" derived from Revelation[58] leaves no doubt as to what the Vatican-approved doctrine was at that time. Rome, it is true, did not exactly embark on a vigorous anti-evolution crusade, as did some Protestant denominations. No papal bulls or encyclicals thundered against the novel ideas; but neither did any such 'heavyweight' documents ever condemn Galileo or Copernicus. It is also true (as we saw Fr. Tripepi complain obliquely) that Rome remained silent about some Catholic authors who were propagating the same evolutionary hypotheses as Léroy. However, when specific works such as his landed on Holy Office desks, confronting the Congregation with the need to speak out for or against, the decision was invariably and unambiguously negative.

**2. Regarding Sub-Human Evolution.** In contrast to this firm initial opposition to human evolution, it is not clear that Rome was at any stage anxious to intervene in order to censure the hypothesis of biological evolution *as such*, that is, in reference to the lower, sub-human species. Certainly, there were not lacking theologians, such as Tripepi, who argued from Scripture and Tradition against every form of evolution, that is, in favor of the special creation of *all* organic species; but as early as 1860, the German bishops, in the Church's initial magisterial intervention in the controversy provoked the previous year by the publication of *The Origin of Species*, limited themselves to condemning the hypothesis of a "spontaneous" (i.e., purely natural) evolution of the *human* body. And it seems that the Vatican felt it prudent to follow that lead. Certainly, no public magisterial statement emanating from Rome — whether from the Pontifical Biblical Commission, the Holy Office/CDF, or from a Successor of Peter — has ever up to the present time affirmed that the natural evolution of lower species is incompatible with divine revelation. Of course, if the 'six days' of Creation week are understood literally and historically, this obviously does rule out evolution in any shape or form. But the 'long-ages' geology of Lyell and other scientists predated Darwin's book by several decades, and, by the last thirty to forty years of the nineteenth century, had become so established as a canon of scientific respectability that most Catholic theologians (including the conservative Fr. Tripepi), along with the Biblical Commission itself in 1909, felt constrained to admit a certain openness to the 'day-age' reading of the word *yom* ("day") in *Genesis* 1. (Late 20th- and 21st-century scientific arguments for a young earth were, of course, generally unknown a century ago.)

**3. Regarding the *reasons* for opposing human evolution.** With regard to the origin of the *human* body, the principal doctrinal point the Holy Office was insisting on against Léroy (and, it seems, against Caverni in 1878) was the reality of an immediate divine intervention by which the matter used by God became apt or disposed for the reception of a rational soul. In other words, Léroy's view that the only divine intervention was God's very act of infusing the soul was deemed unorthodox. Such a view was judged contrary to *Genesis* 2: 7, the historical character of which was clearly being upheld by the Holy Office. As Tripepi, its most influential consultor, insisted, not only does the natural sense of the text indicate *two* distinct (even if possibly simultaneous) divine actions — the formation from 'clay' of Adam's body and the 'breathing in' of the life-giving soul — but an unbroken consensus of the Fathers, Doctors and approved theologians interpreted the text in that sense. Léroy's thesis was also open to a philosophical objection: it implied that a purely material, biological process could produce matter that was apt for a spiritual soul; and this would not only be an effect out of all proportion to its causes, but would also seem to call in question the radical distinction between spirit and matter.

**4.Non-condemnation of 'special transformism'.** Given the logic of its tolerant posture toward evolutionary theory as applied to the lower species, the Holy Office could not rule out *a priori* the possibility that natural evolutionary processes might have gone as far as producing hominid creatures whose bodily features approximated those of *homo sapiens*. The increasing insistence of contemporary secular science that such creatures were in fact man's ancestors, confronted by the Church's insistence that an immediate supernatural intervention for the formation of Adam's body was divinely-taught truth, soon produced the compromise or 'concordist' hypothesis that came to be dubbed by Catholic theologians as 'special transformism': the idea that the matter upon which the Creator intervened was not inorganic or inert, but living: that is to say, it consisted of the uniting sperm and ovum of two hominids, which God would have miraculously 'upgraded' so as to render the resulting zygote apt for the infusion of a rational soul. [If such a thing happened, the human zygote was the First Immaculate Conception conceived without Original Sin. How does that work out with the doctrine of the Immaculate Conception?] This scenario was to be distinguished from the 'natural transformism" postulated by the Darwinists and those Catholics strongly influenced by them, such as Fr. Léroy. 'Special transformism' had the seeming advantage of enabling Catholics to say that they could accept human evolution while still upholding the traditional doctrine of a special creation of man by God in both body and soul. This theory was never censured by the Holy Office, and while it has not been explicitly distinguished from natural transformism in 20th-century magisterial statements on evolution, it appears to be what Pope Pius XII had in mind in expressing a cautious and conditional openness, in *Humani Generis*, to the hypothesis that the human body was formed from "pre-existing living matter".

[How rigorously conditioned the "conditional openness" of Pius XII was is explained in Appendix I of this book which includes a analysis of *Humani Generis*. ]


**5. Regarding the first woman.** It is noteworthy that no censure was even necessary, during this period, either of a polygenistic account of human origins or of the thesis that the body of the first *woman* was also a product of evolution. This is because no Catholic author, it seems, had yet dared advocate these theses, in opposition to truths which were so firmly established in Scripture and Tradition. We saw Fr. Tripepi observe that neither Fr. Léroy nor any other contemporary Catholic evolutionists, to the best of his knowledge, were going so far as to question the historicity of God's miraculous formation of Eve from Adam's side as he slept. This truth, after all, in the middle of the historical period under discussion, was reasserted by the Supreme Pontiff himself as an "undoubted" part of "the Church's permanent doctrine" (Encyclical *Arcanum*, February 10, 1880, §5).

\* \* \* \* \* \* \*

Finally, we might ask how relevant today are the Holy Office deliberations and decisions of over a century that we have considered in this paper. I would argue that the hitherto unknown Holy Office consultor Fr. Luigi Tripepi deserves full credit for his forthright refusal to be swayed by the siren-songs of Darwinism, and for his cogent defense of the rock-solid witness from Scripture and Tradition to the immediate divine origin of both Adam's and Eve's bodies. In the light of the much more substantial scientific evidence which is now available against evolution a hundred years later, this Vatican decision based on Tripepi's recommendations seems more relevant and opportune than ever. Nor, it should be added, has this decision against 'natural transformism' as the explanation of human origins ever been reversed by any subsequent decision of the See of Peter. Pope Pius XII's very qualified openness to human evolution in *Humani Generis* shows no signs of extending to any hypothesis more radical than that of 'special transformism', and Pope John Paul II's principal statement on this issue, his 1996 allocution to the Pontifical Academy of Sciences, in its strictly doctrinal statements, manifests his intention simply to confirm what his predecessor had already said in 1950.

But will 'special transformism' itself stand up to scrutiny? Even supposing for the sake of argument that this hypothesis could be shown to be not intrinsically contrary to revealed truth, it seems to suffer from the fatal defect of being totally gratuitous: that is, there is no positive evidence whatever from either revelation or reason to suggest that it is true. Rather, it seems like a desperate attempt to mix together two radically different world-views that cannot blend in with each other any better than oil and water. Precisely because the 'special transformism' scenario postulates a miracle, in the sense of a physical event that is naturally inexplicable, no evolutionary scientist — whether theistic or atheistic — would ever accept it as having the slightest support from his own discipline. (Indeed, it is very arguable that the whole rationale for believing in evolution in any shape or form is, at bottom, the 'naturalist' philosophical premise that any appeal to miraculous divine interventions at any stage of the molecules-to-man process must be rigorously excluded.) But on the other hand, the *kind* of miracle being postulated in this case finds no more support from revelation than it does from science. Nothing in the Genesis account, or in any other source in Scripture or Tradition, suggests even remotely that God carried out any miracle involving the sperm and ovum of a pair of ape-like, semi-human creatures.

Perhaps, then, the wheel will eventually turn full circle, so that as evolution becomes increasingly discredited, the Catholic theology of the 21st century will return to a belief in the historical truth of that natural and traditional reading of *Genesis* which Fr. Luigi Tripepi and the Holy Office defended in the 19th century: the direct, immediate formation by God of the first man's body from *non-living, inorganic* matter.

---

## ENDNOTES

1. *"Primi parentes a Deo immediate conditi sunt. Itaque Scripturæ sanctæ fideique plane adversantem illorum declaramus sententiam, qui asserere non verentur, spontanea naturæ imperfectioris in perfectiorem continuo ultimoque humanam hanc immutatione hominem, si corpus quidem species, prodidisse"* (Tit. IV, c. 14). The original Latin text is cited in E. C. Messenger, *Evolution and Theology* (New York: Macmillan, 1932, p. 226, n. 1). However the above English translation, which seems to me more accurate than Messenger's, is that found in Patrick O'Connell, *Science of Today*

*and the Problems of Genesis* (2nd. edition of 1968, reprinted by TAN Books [Rockford, Illinois, 1993], p. 187). (By the inclusion of the word "spontaneous," this judgment against evolution stops short of condemning the hypothesis of 'special transformism'.)

2. This information is found in the Holy Office archive *Acta Congregationis ab anno 1894 ad annum 1896*, recorded by the Secretary, Rev. Fr. Cicognani, IIa; 132; p.71. (The translation from the French original is by the present writer.)

3. Ibid. The Decree in question was actually issued in 1633.

4. Ibid., p. 82.

5. Ibid., pp. 25-26. This and all subsequent citations in this article have been translated by the present writer. The originals are in Italian except where otherwise stated.

6. Ibid., p. 90.

7. *Acta*, op. cit., p. 118.

8. Ibid.

9. Ibid.

10. Op. cit., p. 123, IVa.

11. Tripepi's privately printed opusculum, included in the file with the *Acta*, simply bears the title of Léroy's book, and takes the form of a letter addressed to the Cardinals of the Congregation: "Most Eminent Fathers, . . . ".

12. Domenichelli, p. 3.

13. Cf. ibid., pp. 5-6.

14. Cf. ibid., p. 8.

15. Cf. ibid., pp. 10-11.

16. Ibid., p. 12.

17. Cf. ibid., p. 13.

18. Cf. ibid., p. 15.

19. Cf. ibid., pp. 15-16.

20. Cited, ibid., p. 19 (Translated from French original, at Léroy's p. 256, cited by Domenichelli).

21. Cf. ibid., pp. 20-21. Domenichelli goes on to note (p. 23) that the purely natural theory of human evolution condemned at Cologne was also qualified as "heretical" by the great German theologian Matthias Scheeben (in *Dogmatica*, Book III, n. 384).

22. Ibid., p. 21.

23. *"C'est par son insufflation que le Createur a trasformé le limon en chair humaine"*, cited from Léroy's p. 261 by Domenichelli, op,

cit., p. 21.

24. Ibid., pp. 22-23.

25. Ibid., p. 24.

26. Ibid., p. 23.

27. Ibid.

28. Ibid., p. 25. St. Thomas' affirmation of an "immediate" formation of the human body, in order to be compatible with his admission of this possibility of an angelic "ministry", must be understood to mean that such formation was beyond the intrinsic or proper capacity of any created power. Thus, Aquinas would appear to mean that although no angel by its own power could form the first human body, an angel might have been an instrumental "minister" whereby the divine power produced that effect. In the same way, one could say that even when God uses a saint as his "minister" to work a miracle, that is still an "immediate" action of God, in contrast to "mediate" actions in which the intrinsic powers of God's creatures produce their natural effects, according to His will.

29. Ibid.

30. Domenichelli, p. 25.

31. Tripepi, op. cit., p.2.

32. Ibid., p. 8.

33. Cf. ibid., p. 9.

34. Cf. ibid., p. 10.

35. Ibid., p. 11. Here Tripepi refers to the authority of Cardinal Camillo Mazzella, a noted Roman theologian of the late 19th century.

36. Cf. ibid., pp. 21-22.

37. Cf. ibid., p. 23.

38. Ibid., p. 25.

39. Ibid., p. 12.

40. St. George Mivart, a lay British biology professor, was, it seems, the first Catholic scholar ever to attempt a reconciliation between human evolution and the faith of his Church. His books *The Genesis of Species* (London, 1871) and *Lessons From Nature* (London, 1876) were placed by the Vatican on the *Index of Forbidden Books* (cf. V. Zubizarreta, *Theologia Dogmatica Scholastica*, Vol. II [Bilbao: Eléxpura, 1926], p. 479, n. 5).

41. Ibid., p. 14.

42. Cf. ibid., p. 15.

43. Cf. ibid., pp. 15-16.
44. Ibid., p. 17.
45. Ibid., p. 18.
46. Cf. ibid., p. 19.
47. Ibid., p. 20.
48. Cf. ibid., p. 26.
49. Cf. ibid., p. 27.
50. Cf. ibid., pp. 29-31.
51. Ibid., p. 44.
52. Ibid.
53. Cf. ibid., pp. 50-51.
54. Cf. ibid., pp. 52-53.
55. Cf. ibid., p. 54.
56. Cf. Zubizarreta, op. cit., (see note 40 above), p. 479, note 6.
57. Cited in G. Van Noort, *De Deo Creatore*, 2nd edn. (Amsterdam: Van Langenhuysen, 1912), pp. 114-115, note 1).
58. Cf. C. Mazzella, *De Deo Creante*, 4th edn. (Rome: Forzani, 1896): *"Primi parentes,* **prout ex divina revelatione constat,** *non modo quoad animam,* **sed etiam quoad corpus, immediate a Deo conditi sunt.** . . . **Quam certissimam veritatem** *frustra evertere aut infirmare nituntur qui nunc audiant Transformistæ"* (pp. 353-354, emphasis added).

THAT IS THE END OF FR. HARRISON'S ARTICLE

---

Not mentioned in Fr. Harrison's research was the 1884 encyclical *Humanum Genus* (On Freemasonry and Naturalism). Pope Leo XIII explained how Naturalists and Freemasons would use schools to integrate evolution into philosophy to the detriment of morality and culture.

The Magisterium's rejection of evolution at the end of the 19th Century as explained above continued into the early 20th Century as one can see from Pope St. Pius X's 1907 encyclical *Pascendi Dominici Gregis* (On the Doctrine of the Modernists). Note how he connected belief in evolution with Modernism, which he described as "the synthesis of all heresies."

> First of all [the Modernists] lay down the general principle that in a living religion everything is subject to change, and must in fact be changed. In this way they pass to what is practically their principal doctrine, namely, evolution. To the laws of evolution everything is subject.

Phillip Campbell, on his blog *Unam Sanctam Catholicam*, explained the reason Modernism is the synthesis of all heresies is not because it professes all heresies formally, but because of its incorporation of the principle of evolution as applied to truth. Darwin had presented the world with a model of reality which stressed becoming over being; in fact, there really was no "being" in the Aristotelian-Thomist sense. Every "being" was merely a moment in the history of becoming. That being the case, it was only so long before this concept was applied to revealed truth and even God Himself, and thus the Modernist theological school proposed that dogma can in fact evolve, not just in expression but in substance, which is a logical consequent of affirming the evolution of material substances. This is the sense in which Modernism is a synthesis of all heresies: because truth itself is subject to change, dogma becomes a potent medium for the impression of *any* teaching. Once the evolution of dogma is admitted, every heresy is present in potency.

So, how did evolution, identified as the underpinning of the Modernist heresy by the Magisterium at the beginning of the 20th Century, become mainstream in Catholic circles at the end of that century? Hugh Owen, Director of the Kolbe Center for the Study of Creation, has explained how evolution began to infiltrate Catholic thinking.

> Contrary to popular belief in the English-speaking world, Charles Darwin was not nearly as successful a propagandist

for microbe-to-man evolution as his German colleague Ernst Haeckel, author of the fraudulent drawings used to "prove" the common descent of all of the different kinds of creatures from a "primitive" one-celled common ancestor.

In his 1868 book *Natürliche Schöpfungsgeschichte* (The History of Natural Creation) Ernst Haeckel suggested that he had made various comparisons using human, monkey and dog embryos. The drawings he produced consisted of nearly identical embryos. On the basis of these drawings, Haeckel then suggested that the life forms involved had common origins. An exceptionally good and well-researched article (by a Muslim) that explains the fraud in detail and its enormous influence on biology and physiology education that should be read is here: https://www.harunyahya.com/en/Articles/19164/haeckels-embryo-drawings-are-fraudulent

Haeckel's bogus "proof" was the single most effective piece of propaganda in the campaign to convince the intellectual elite of the Western world that microbe-to-man evolution was a scientific fact rather than a wild conjecture. Hugh Owen explained how the fraud began its spread into mainstream Catholic education

> It convinced Catholic intellectuals from [American] Fr. John Augustine Zahm at Notre Dame at the dawn of the twentieth century to [German] Fr. Karl Rahner towards the end of the twentieth century that the traditional teaching of the Church on the special creation of Adam and Eve had been falsified by this "scientific" discovery. Haeckel himself acknowledged how quickly the intellectual elite of the Catholic Church changed its position on evolution.

Fr. Zahm (1851-1921) was a professor of physics at ND. His 1896 book, *Evolution and Dogma*, was very influential. In this text, as in his others, Zahm argued that Roman Catholicism could fully accept an evolutionary view of biological systems, as long as this view was not centered around Darwin's theory of natural selection. After the

Vatican censured the book in 1898, Zahm fully accepted this rebuttal and pulled away from any writing concerning the relationship of theology and science. His obedience notwithstanding, Fr. Zahm's book and theology remained a fixture in Notre Dame's teaching by a faculty that accepted Darwinism as a proved fact. It was used throughout the Catholic higher education system. I found it in the library of a self-described "orthodox" college that has a large collection of books promoting both atheistic and theistic evolution. The book is still available from that giant online book seller.

Fr. Karl Rahner (1904-1984), a Jesuit, was one of the most influential theologians of the 20th century. His 6-volume *Theological Investigations* was a staple in seminaries around the world and did enormous harm.

In his 1906 book, *Last Words on Evolution,* Haeckel observed
> ...the interesting efforts that the Church has lately made to enter into a peaceful compromise with its deadly enemy, Monistic science. It has decided to accept to a certain extent, and to accommodate to its creed (in a distorted and mutilated form) the doctrine of evolution, which it has vehemently opposed for thirty years. This remarkable change of front on the part of the Church militant seemed to me so interesting and important, and at the same time so misleading and mischievous ... Our science of evolution won its greatest triumph when, at the beginning of the twentieth century, its most powerful opponents, the Churches, became reconciled to it, and endeavored to bring their dogmas into line with it.

Haeckel could not have been referring to the Magisterium when he referred to "the Church" because as we have seen, it wasn't the Pope or Vatican Congregations who accepted evolution. It was the clerical intellectuals. Hugh Owen added that "Haeckel went on to note the unique role played by scientists within the Society of Jesus in accomplishing this revolution against the "foundations" of the Creed. Haeckel wrote:

> The Jesuit Father Wasmann, and his colleagues, have - unwittingly - done a very great service to the progress of pure science. The Catholic Church, the most powerful and widespread of the Christian sects, sees itself compelled to capitulate to the idea of evolution. It embraces the most important application of the idea, Lamarck and Darwin's theory of descent, which it had vigorously combated until twenty years ago. It does, indeed, mutilate the great tree, cutting off its roots and its highest branch; it rejects spontaneous generation or archigony at the bottom, and the descent of man from animal ancestors above. But these exceptions will not last. Impartial biology will take no notice of them, and the religious creed will at length determine that the more complex species have been evolved from a series of simpler forms according to Darwinian principles . . . The open acknowledgment of [the truth of evolution by the Jesuit, Father Wasmann, deserves careful attention, and we may look forward to a further development. If his force of conviction and his moral courage are strong enough, he will go on to draw the normal conclusions from his high scientific attainments and leave the Catholic Church, as the prominent Jesuits, Count Hoensbroech and the able geologist, Professor Renard of Ghent, one of the workers on the deep-sea deposits in the *Challenger* expedition, have lately done. But even if this does not happen, his recognition of Darwinism, in the name of Christian belief, will remain a landmark in the history of evolution. His ingenious and very Jesuitical attempt to bring together the opposite poles will have no very mischievous effect; it will rather tend to hasten the victory of the scientific conception of evolution over the mystic beliefs of the Churches.

Hugh Owen pointed out that

52

With this statement Haeckel showed keen insight into the weakness of theistic evolutionist attempts to reconcile molecules-to-man evolution with the antithetical dogma of creation. He rightly anticipated that if Catholic theologians accepted the naturalistic accounts of Darwin and his disciples for the origin of man and other living things and abandoned the constant teaching of the Church on the fundamental doctrine of creation, thoughtful Catholics would realize the absurdity of trying to reconcile these opposites. He realized that theologians who allowed natural scientists to dictate to them in regard to the dogma of creation would end up ceding the primacy of theology as the Queen of the Sciences and allow Natural Science to usurp her place. Haeckel also noted the irony that Jesuits and other Catholic apologists for theistic evolution at the end of the nineteenth century tried to make it seem as if the Church had "admitted the theory of evolution for decades" when just a decade or two before the Church had been united against evolution as a mortal threat to the very foundations of the Faith.

Haeckel, in continuing his verbal "victory lap," commented on another Jesuit of note:

We find a similar diplomatic retreat in the popular work of the Jesuit, Father Martin Gander, *The Theory of Descent* (1904): "Thus the modern forms of matter were not immediately created by God; they are effects of the formative forces, which were put by the creator in the primitive matter, and gradually came into view in the course of the earth's history, when the external conditions were given in the proper combination." That is a remarkable change of front on the part of the clergy.

George Tyrrell (1861-1909) and Alfred Loisy (1857-1940), were among other Jesuits who, because of their acceptance of evolution, specialized in the rejection of any idea of supernatural revelation. It is most probable that "evolution is a proved fact" was taught in all of those once great Jesuit universities which, like those in the U.S., (Georgetown, Marquette, Boston College) have become leaders in heterodox Catholicism. According his testimony, once famous university and seminary biblical professor and author, Vincentian priest Bruce Vawter, he was taught that evolution was completely compatible with Catholicism at the seminary in the 1940s. His popular 1956 book, *A Path Through Genesis*, had an enormous impact in the theological community leading them to the common belief that evolution happened but "God did it" and the Divine Revelation of Genesis is what? According to Bishop Barron, chairman of the U.S. Bishops' Committee for Catechetics and Evangelization, it is not the historical narrative it seems; it is "theology, mysticism, spirituality; a theological reflection on the origin of all things." As will be related later, sisters, brothers, and priests in the 1950's were teaching students high-school students to believe in evolution.

The late evolutionist Harvard professor Stephen Jay Gould, in a 1983 article "The Hardening of the Modern Synthesis," wrote that in technical papers of the 1940s, the modern Darwinian orthodoxy had not yet congealed and a style of doubt remained quite common among evolutionary biologists. He said evolution only coalesced as the hardline orthodoxy in the 1950s and 1960s. But apparently many Catholic clergy and educators were "on board" before that.

Today's Catholic priests and lay intellectuals who hold to theistic evolution came up through the same education systems which taught them to believe in evolution, and there were no counter voices. They had no reason to doubt it or even think critically about it. In many seminaries the students' belief was reinforced by Scripture studies following the "scientific method" of Bultmann, based on evolution as explained by Cardinal Ratzinger and quoted earlier in this book. A pastor in the Diocese of Arlington, Virginia, wrote in "The Catholic Thing" blog in July 2017:

> In the 1980s, I attended a Midwest seminary that was schizophrenic with respect to the Faith. ... Scripture studies were essentially liberal Protestant. ... One of the Scripture professors, Father Otto, was ... a disciple of Rudolf Bultmann, the famous (or, as I prefer, the infamous) liberal Protestant theologian whose scholarly technique of "demythologizing" Scriptures corrupted generations of students. Since our Scripture studies were essentially divorced from the Catholic faith, it was only natural that we allowed Protestant seminarians to attend classes.

While all ranks of the clergy from Pope Francis on down appear to be caught up into believing God used evolution to create us in a multi-billion-year process of evolution, Evangelicals recognized it was philosophy, not science. As related in chapter 2, when world-famous evolution promoter Richard Dawkins was asked what caused him to disbelieve in God's existence he replied:

> Oh well, by far the most important I suppose was understanding evolution. I think the Evangelical Christians have really got it right, it in a way, in seeing evolution as the enemy, whereas the more, what shall we say, sophisticated theologians who are quite happy to live with evolution, I think they are deluded. I think the Evangelicals have got it right in that there really is a deep incompatibility between evolution and Christianity and I think I realized that at about the age of 16.

The first organized scientific opposition to Darwinian orthodoxy in the United States began in 1970 when Evangelicals founded the Institute for Creation Research (ICR.org). Scientific, theological, and philosophical opposition to dogmatic Darwinism, although still at a relatively low level, is sufficiently visible in the "internet age" that most theistic evolutionists ought to be aware that it exists. But a variety of factors, including the fear of being labelled "anti-scientific," holds back many from examination of the lack of evidence and the sheer improbability of the evolution theory. Also, a fair number of Catholic clergy "look down their noses' at their stereotype of a "bible-thumping fundamentalist." As a result, many continue to misunderstand the controversy about their very origins. One particular group of intellectuals within the Catholic culture that refuses to face up to the lack of evidence for and the theological implication of their belief in evolution subscribes to "Thomistic Evolution." They hold that evolution is compatible with the teaching of Thomas Aquinas. That movement is spearheaded by 4 Dominicans who received enhanced exposure to the "scientific consensus" while earning advanced technical degrees. Another Dominican, Fr. Michael Chaberek, published a comprehensive refutation of "Thomistic Evolution" in *Aquinas and Evolution* by quoting the actual writings of Aquinas. At the beginning of his book, he raised the same question about how evolution became mainstream. He started out by noting that since the beginning of the 20$^{th}$ century, when evolution was soundly refuted by Popes and theologians of Vatican Congregations, neither evolution theory nor Catholic doctrine has changed. So how and why did belief in evolution, that was soundly refuted at the beginning of the 20$^{th}$ century, become mainstream in Catholic academia by the end of the 20$^{th}$ century? He answered:

> As we noted, it is not the understanding of Aquinas or evolution that has changed over the last century or so. It is rather the change in paradigms—from roughly speaking 'Biblical' or 'creationist' to 'naturalistic' or 'evolutionary'. This change of paradigms explains why a great number of today's Thomists greatly differ from those of a century ago. In our opinion, the 'evolutionary' as opposed to the 'Biblical' is not the proper context in which the problem of origins should be addressed. For this reason, we believe that not today's, but the previous Thomists were closer to the truth

regarding both—the interpretation of Aquinas's metaphysics and the assessment of the evolutionary theory of origins…

In what follows we will show that the teachings of Thomas Aquinas—and indeed any sound philosophy…are not just incompatible with the Darwinian theory but exclude it in principle. By showing this, we want to achieve another objective, namely, to help contemporary Thomists to realize some of the difficulties, inaccuracies, or even flat-out errors in their interpretation of Aquinas when it comes to the origin of species and man.

In the pontificate of Francis, traditional orthodox Catholics around the world writhe in spiritual pain over the series of statements and documents coming from Rome. They see both subtle and radical shifts in matters that were considered moral certitudes for 2000 years, but with no explicable reasoning behind the shifts. They are just "evolving." The Pope felt no need to explain them although many begged him to do so. I'm not saying these "shifts" are examples of evolution-based modernism, because "who am I to judge," but when Cardinals submitted formal requests to the Pope to clarify his meaning, e.g., the *Dubia*, it may be that they saw it as such.

From his non-authoritative public statements, it is evident that Pope Francis believes God created through cosmic and biological evolution. Many, if not most, of his fellow Jesuits have been trapped in a 19th century science time warp since the heyday of Pierre Teilhard de Chardin, S.J., the French author of evolution theology fiction. He was trained as a paleontologist and geologist. As a member of a paleontology dig in 1913, he discovered a canine tooth that sealed the evidence that a fossil found in an English gravel pit the previous year was the missing link in the evolution of humans from an animal. That fact gave his evolution theology fiction enormous prestige and credibility within the Jesuits. The fossil, known as Piltdown Man, was displayed in the British Museum until 1953, when it was a judged to be a complete fraud. But during the four decades it was displayed in the British Museum it was also in science textbooks worldwide with highly-imaginative artist's conceptual renderings as a half-animal, half-man, based on just a fossil skull, jawbone, and tooth. At least two generations of Jesuits and school children (including future seminary professors, bishops and popes such as Benedict XVI, JP II, and Francis) studied it and believed it was a fact. Who knows how much that fraud contributed to the wayward theology of so many clergy because faith in evolution has consequences?

The Bible, as the Church teaches, is inerrant. But when *Genesis* is interpreted to conform to the "faux science" of evolution theory, paragraph 282 of the *Catechism of the Catholic Church* is not being taken seriously and implemented. School children want to know where we come from and where we are going. And the explanation from parents and Catholic educators has to be more than the dumbed-down intellectual level found in CCD programs or "holy books" that pass for Catholic education. And telling them God actually guided the billion-year random process they learned in science class is apparently not working. The vacuum created by the failure to teach reason-based Catholic creationism has been filled by the secular Humanists with their assertion of cosmic and biological evolution that renders God unnecessary. Richard Dawkins has explained to millions of his followers that "Darwin made it possible to be an intellectually fulfilled atheist."

More than half of U.S. adults view science and faith as being "often in conflict." Given the weight and prestige of science in our culture, that puts faith in a corner. Simple affirmations in favor of religious tradition or naïve apologetic approaches won't suffice — not least with young people as they encounter a range of challenging viewpoints.

# Chapter 5
# Supernaturalism and Naturalism

There is no question that the Catholic supernatural doctrines of creation are based solely on faith and not on scientific proof. However, that faith is based on what we claim to believe is Divine Revelation either from Scripture or our Sacred Tradition. Further, our faith is supported by philosophical reasoning, an intellectual capability we also believe only humans possess because we are "made in the image and likeness of God." We also believe that miracles do happen. God is not a distant "watchmaker" who designed and wound it all up; He is a loving Father who intervenes in His creation. We don't try to 'prove' the Bible with science; rather, we accept the Bible's propositions as true without proof, i.e., as axioms. *All* philosophical systems, not just Christianity, start with *axioms*. There are good reasons for accepting the axioms of Scripture as true, because it can be shown that they lead to a consistent view of physical and moral reality, which other axioms can't provide.

In *Aquinas and Evolution*, Thomistic scholar Fr. Michael Chaberek observed that abstract philosophical arguments for the existence of God are

> more certain and permanent than scientific ones. Scientific arguments, however, are more concrete and easier to grasp for those who have not possessed the ability of abstract thinking. And this is why the persuasive power of the scientific arguments for ID often turns out to be greater than the philosophical arguments for the existence of God. And this is why ID creates more resistance among unbelievers than any of the five ways [of proving God's existence] proposed by Aquinas.

Our Catholic youth can be taught the faith-affirming facts of natural science to counter the faith-destroying propaganda of the Humanists dogma of evolution. But it is a job that must be organized, led and encouraged at the parish level. Can we get parish priests to facilitate the teaching of faith-affirming natural science? Or will they keep abjuring to their DREs who will keep doing conventional CCD that has failed for the last half century?

What too many Catholic teachers don't know, or if they heard it, don't accept it, is that evolution is based solely on faith and not on scientific proof. The leading lights in evolutionary science know it is all speculation, but are unwilling to call it a faith. They say that when any aspect of the evolutionary hypothesis is proven to be untrue or downright implausible, as long as it is replaced by another hypothesis, it is still science. Occasionally, though, a top-tier evolution-believing scientist of impeccable reputation in his community will let "the cat out of the bag," so to speak. An example of such an evolutionist is Richard Lewontin.

Richard Lewontin (b. 1929) is another of the New York city-born sons of Eastern European Jews who became famous evolutionists. Carl Sagan (agnostic) and Stephen Jay Gould (atheist, Marxist) were more famous because they were also media personalities but Lewontin (atheist, Marxist) was a more "heavyweight" academic. Dr. Lewontin's field is evolutionary biology and evolutionary population genetics which in 1966 he combined into evolutionary molecular genetics. Lewontin held an endowed chair in zoology and biology at Harvard for 25 years. He collaborated with Gould and another atheist that the *New York Times* called the "Darwin of the 20th Century," Ernst Mayr. They were all at Harvard during most of their careers. On January 9, 1997, Professor Lewontin published in *The New York Review* [of Books] a review of Carl Sagan's *The Demon-Haunted World: Science as a Candle in the Dark*. The review article was

"Billions and billions of demons." The words in italics were in italics in Lewontin's original:

> Our willingness to accept scientific claims that are against common sense is the key to an understanding of the real struggle between science and the supernatural. We take the side of science in spite of the patent absurdity of some of its constructs, *in spite* of its failure to fulfill many of its extravagant promises of health and life, *in spite* of the tolerance of the scientific community for unsubstantiated just-so stories, because we have a prior commitment, a commitment to materialism.
>
> It is not that the methods and institutions of science somehow compel us to accept a material explanation of the phenomenal world, but, on the contrary, that we are forced by our *a priori* adherence to material causes to create an apparatus of investigation and a set of concepts that produce material explanations, no matter how counter-intuitive, no matter how mystifying to the uninitiated. Moreover, that materialism is absolute, for we cannot allow a Divine Foot in the door. The eminent Kant scholar Lewis Beck used to say that anyone who could believe in God could believe in anything. To appeal to an omnipotent deity is to allow that at any moment the regularities of nature may be ruptured, that Miracles may happen.

If even the evolutionists know deep down inside themselves that their science is really a faith choice that is a religion, how, one may wonder, did evolution become the most accepted story of our origins in America which was, at least until lately, thought of as "a Christian country?" The answer to that question was outlined in the previous chapter but is also described in more historical detail than might have been necessary in chapter 14 of my previous book, *Creation, Evolution, and Catholicism: A Discussion for Those Who Believe*. A pivotal event in that history was the publication in 1933 of *The*

*Humanist Manifesto* and signed by some leading men of that era. The Humanists described themselves as a new religion, that is, a religious movement meant to transcend and replace deity-based religions:

> While this age does owe a vast debt to the traditional religions, it is none the less obvious that any religion that can hope to be a synthesizing and dynamic force for today must be shaped for the needs of this age. To establish such a religion is a major necessity of the present. It is a responsibility which rests upon this generation. We therefore affirm the following:
>
> First: Religious humanists regard the universe as self-existing and not created.
> Second: Humanism believes that man is a part of nature and that he has emerged as the result of a continuous process.
> Third: Holding an organic view of life, humanists find that the traditional dualism of mind and body must be rejected.

In other words, the universe, including all of the matter and energy, always existed, life "emerged" on its own, humans then evolved, and the mind is material just as the body is. No room here for spiritual souls. Those are just the first three of fourteen "affirmations of faith" in that creed-like document.

Humanist philosophy, anchored on materialist origin speculations, is as old as the famous Greeks of the pre-Christian era but it lacked a basis to plausibly refute the Bible's Divine Revelation. Humanist philosophers in Europe labored mightily to supersede the scholastic philosophy of Church Doctors, who developed it in harmony with the Magisterium. Two books of a scientific gloss, written by Charles Lyell (evolutionary geology) and Charles Darwin (evolutionary biology), appeared in the 19th Century and pumped new life into Humanism by advancing theories to explain scientifically-observed data by materialistic inference.

In his book, *The Genesis of a Humanist Manifesto*, Edwin H. Wilson, one of the founders and preeminent leaders of the Humanist movement, explained how evolutionary cosmology and biological evolution undergird Humanism. Wilson wrote that "Humanism came of age in 1933 with the publication of *Humanist Manifesto I*." Wilson stated that its affirmations of faith regarding cosmology, biological and cultural evolution, human nature, epistemology, ethics, religion, self-fulfillment, and the quest for freedom and social justice described precisely "the leading ideas and aspirations of its era." That was no idle boast. Edwin Wilson correctly observed that *The Humanist Manifesto* reflected the reality that by 1933 "what was conceived by the convergence of freethought and religious liberalism at the end of the 19th century" had come to reign in the universities, if not yet in the local school houses. Anyone reviewing the list of that *Manifesto's* signers might recognize the name of John Dewey, the most influential philosopher in American history. Dewey's role in transmitting the Humanist religion nationally and internationally as an author and as a professor (Michigan, Chicago, and Columbia) between 1886 and 1939 to the leading intellectuals and the professional educators of that age is detailed in *Creation, Evolution, and Catholicism: A Discussion for Those Who Believe*. Dewey wrote in 1908:

> Bearing in mind the losses and inconveniences of our time as best we may it is the part of men to labor persistently and patiently for the clarification and development of the positive creed of life implicit in democracy and in science, and to work for the transformation of all practical instrumentalities of education until they are in harmony with these ideas.

Dewey was singularly successful in helping to transform "all practical instrumentalities of education" to be in harmony with the ideas of secular Humanism. The first three faith affirmations of the *Humanist Manifesto* regarding cosmic and biological evolution and the purely material nature of man has been the practical Creed of the American education industry, even if many or most educators never heard of it.

63

Dennis Q. McInerny, when he was professor of philosophy at Our Lady of Guadalupe, the Priestly Fraternity of St. Peter's Seminary in Nebraska, wrote in a review of *Creation, Evolution, and Catholicism* that:

> Anyone who still would have the temerity to make the bold proclamation that evolution is a fact is clearly out of the swim of things, and innocently unaware of what's really going on today in the world of science, biological science in particular. Unfortunately, there is a very large discrepancy between the actual status of evolutionary theory, with the many serious problems by which it is beset, and what children and young people are being taught in our schools, very much including Catholic and many other Christian schools. Whether educators have simply not gotten the word regarding how evolution now actually stands (i.e., tottering), or they have gotten the word and refuse to accept it because of their firmly held ideological biases, the disconcerting fact of the matter is that they continue to teach evolutionary theory (in a necessarily carefully doctored way) as if it were a coherent system composed of rock-solid scientific truths. It is anything but that, and educators are doing a deep disservice to their charges, and to society at large, by persistently promulgating as hard science what in truth is as soft as a gentle spring rain in the west of Ireland, and also like that rain, it might be added, it is all wet.

# Chapter 6
# Can We Save Our Gen Z Catholics?

Catholics have no scientific proof for our faith so our adolescents are being peeled away by the claims of another faith that convinces the kids that it is scientifically proved. What can we do about this? We can't prove our faith by science, but we can use real empirical modern science to disprove or show how implausible that other faith is. The Evangelicals, according to Christian Smith's decades-long research, have been far more successful in the religious education of their children than Catholics have. And he presents the data to prove that.

Why is that so? In 1933 Humanists launched the religious movement meant to transcend and replace deity-based religions. The majority of Catholic intellectuals sought accommodation but Evangelicals fought back intellectually. Starting in the 1970s, Evangelicals who were well-credentialed in most of the various disciplines of science began the creation-science movement. The movement's purpose is to deconstruct through modern science the evolutionary tale from the 19th century that supports Humanism. In 1990, agnostic scientists who rejected the supposed mechanisms of evolution as implausible explanations of the order and design in the living world joined in by founding the Seattle-based Discovery Institute. Those scientists call their work the Intelligent Design Movement. Their goal is to convince the scientific community about what their research tells them, namely, that the world was purposefully designed by an intelligence. It did not happen by chance. They maintain no public position on by what, when, or why it was designed so they are not "creationists" in the religious sense of that word. Privately, many are men of faith such as Christians and Jews.

The evolution story advances: "primordial slime, simple animals, complex animals...". In school the microscopic-size bacteria and the one-cell ameba help to illustrate the "simple" beginning of evolution. What modern science has discovered and creationist and intelligent design scientists are promulgating is that what was said to be "simple," because it was tiny and scientists of an earlier age did not know the complexity of their inner workings, is far from simple. Biochemist Michael Denton, M.D., Ph.D., published *Evolution: A Theory in Crisis* in 1985. In it he presented a systematic critique of Neo-Darwinism ranging from paleontology, fossils, homology, molecular biology, genetics, and biochemistry.

Michael Behe, a Catholic and professor of biochemistry at Lehigh University, once fully accepted the theory of evolution. In his 2019 book, *Darwin Devolves*, he related that in his K–12 Catholic education, Sister Marie taught her class that "the best evidence these days shows that evolution is correct" (p. 6). After reading Denton's book, he came to question evolution. Based on his research he found that even the smallest "simple" living things involve "irreducible complexity" that could not have resulted from any of the mechanisms proposed as explanations of evolution. For example, plankton is a generic term for small marine creatures such as algae, bacteria, and protozoa. Although tiny, they are packed with incredibly intricate submicroscopic structures. This complexity isn't surprising since many of these entities are photosynthetic, able to turn light energy into sugars needed for life's energy. Subsequently Behe wrote a best-selling book called *Darwin's Black Box*. Electrical engineers may refer to a system as a "black box" to mean that one may specify the needed input to and output from a system and leave the designing of the system to another. Darwin could see what "simple" living things could do but had no idea about the complexity within the "box."

Dr. Denton made this prediction in his 1985 book:

> It would be an illusion to think that what we are aware of at present is any more than a fraction of the full extent of biological design. In practically every field of fundamental

biological research ever-increasing levels of design and complexity are being revealed at an ever-increasing rate. The credibility of natural selection is weakened, therefore, not only by the perfection we have already glimpsed but by the expectation of further as yet undreamt depths of ingenuity and complexity.

What Dr. Denton wrote in 1985 has certainly come to pass more than he imagined. Engineers have developed a whole new field called biophotonics, bringing light to the life sciences. As just one example, they have invented super-resolution microscopy that enables life science researchers to observe dynamic biological processes inside living cells with unprecedented clarity.

Dr. Denton described himself as an agnostic who rejects biblical creationism. Dr Denton, even as a non-Christian outside observer to the creation/evolution debate, understood the centrality of *Genesis*:

As far as Christianity was concerned, the advent of the theory of evolution and the elimination of traditional teleological thinking was catastrophic. The suggestion that life and man are the result of chance is incompatible with the biblical assertion of their being the direct result of intelligent creative activity. Despite the attempt by liberal theology to disguise the point, the fact is that no biblically derived religion can really be compromised with the fundamental assertion of Darwinian Theory. Chance and design are antithetical concepts, and the decline of religious belief can probably be attributed more to the propagation and advocacy by the intellectual and scientific community of the Darwinian version of evolution than to any other single factor.

Alienation of Catholic youth is taking place "under our noses" in schools every day and it takes a non-Christian to point it out. But Evangelicals have "gotten the message" that 21st century science has sent. A social phenomenon that is practically unknown in the Catholic community is that creationist and intelligent design scientists are crisscrossing our country giving lectures to large crowds in churches and other facilities of Evangelical Christians at the invitations of the pastors. Hundreds of such lectures are on YouTube. Creation Ministries International, the Institute for Creation Research, and the Discovery Institute are the most active and effective. On a much smaller scale the Kolbe Center for the Study of Creation is reaching some Catholic audiences. And what has been proved is that when evolution theory is taught side-by-side with creationist or intelligent design theory, students find the latter two more plausible than evolution and it seals their Christian faith in the Bible's truth.

The Humanists rage against that result! They can't prevent contra-evolution education on church property but will never permit it in a any public venue such as a public school. One would think that Humanists and other believers in evolution would welcome the side-by-side comparison in the schoolroom since they see their faith-science to be superior. But Humanists have preferred to fight that battle in the courtroom. At least two states, Arkansas and Louisiana, and numerous individual school districts have passed "equal time" or "freedom to teach" type statutes or policies, but the Humanists always take it to court as a "separation of church and state" issue based on the First Amendment clause that says "Congress shall make no law respecting an establishment of religion, or prohibiting the free exercise thereof." It might seem quite a stretch to see a requirement that competing science explanations be available to public school students is a violation of the Constitution, but as recent history has demonstrated over and over, there is always a judge to be found known to subvert the law to his ideological preference. Arkansas, and later Louisiana, lost in Court as judges cited the testimony of witnesses that evolutionism is science and contra- evolution, creation-supporting science is just religion. In the Arkansas case, the judge said evolution was science because it was open to revising its theories but creation-supporting science was religion because it had already reached its conclusion.

One of the key witnesses produced by the ACLU lawyers in the 1982 Arkansas case was Michael Ruse, who was a professor of philosophy and zoology at the University of Guelph, Canada. His courtroom testimony loftily dismissed the claim that evolution was an anti-god religion. However, based on an article he wrote for the *National Post*, May 13, 2000, called "How evolution became a religion: creationists correct?", Professor Michael Ruse knew that in fact evolution is an anti-God religion even as he perjured himself under oath in the Arkansas court case. He wrote:

> Evolution is promoted by its practitioners as more than mere science. Evolution is promulgated as an ideology, a secular religion—a full-fledged alternative to Christianity, with meaning and morality. I am an ardent evolutionist and an ex-Christian, but I must admit that in this one complaint—and Mr. Gish [the late Dr. Duane Gish of the Institute for Creation Research] is but one of many to make it—the literalists are absolutely right. Evolution is a religion. This was true of evolution in the beginning, and it is true of evolution still today. … Evolution therefore came into being as a kind of secular ideology, an explicit substitute for Christianity.

None of the leaders in the contra- evolution camp has ever suggested that their theories should replace evolution theory in the schools, even Christian schools, or in taxpayer-funded institutions such as museums or any other venue that touches on origins theory or history. They just seek time to teach students and the public that there are competing scientific theories and that they have the right to know that.

How do those creationist and intelligent design scientists so successfully deconstruct the faux scientific evolution story? Recall that a zombie is something dead that is still walking around. The popular teaching of cosmic and biological evolution that kids get in school and from the popular culture is filled with so many scientifically dead and implausible "proofs" of "evolution" that are still "walking" around in the education system that they are "zombies."

Because Catholic children are taught to believe in these "zombies," we must bury the zombies by teaching the modern natural science that will fasten their faith to their soul. Here is why creation-science or intelligent design science fastens belief in God. In his book, *Darwin's Doubt: The Explosion of Animal Life and the Case for Intelligent Design,* its author Stephen Meyer of the Discovery Institute made a compelling case against evolution on scientific grounds. Toward the end of the book, after he has explained why intelligent design is a scientific theory superior to the various variations of Darwinism, Meyer made this final point:

> The theory of intelligent design is not based on religious belief, nor does it provide a proof for the existence of God. But it does have faith-affirming implications precisely because it suggests the design that we observe in the natural world is real, just as a traditional theistic view of the world would lead us to expect. Of course, that by itself is not a reason to accept the theory. But having accepted it for other reasons, it may be a reason to find it important.

Dr. Meyer's point is that teaching our children zombie-free modern natural science along with our creation doctrines based on reading *Genesis* as the historical narrative that it is would be more effective in saving their faith than trying to "baptize" the materialistic evolution creation myth with the assertion that it is true but "God did it." When we teach modern natural science, we will simultaneously bury the scientific zombies that our kids believe in which are detriments to their faith in the personal Creator God of the Bible.

# Chapter 7
## Bury the Zombies

The famous Orthodox Jew, intellectual, and commentator Michael Medved has written that

> On TV and in the movies, zombies are simultaneously scary and comedic. Zombie science is even more frightening and, at times, even more laughable—and worthy of exposure and ridicule.

In 2000, biologist Jonathan Wells of the Discovery Institute illustrated that so many long-ago discredited evolution stories, that even most evolutionary scientists have abandoned, continued to show up in school textbooks and to be repeated by teachers. They are so patently false but they have been told for so long they have become "icons of evolution" as for example, the Statue of Liberty has become an American patriotic and cultural icon. Wells somewhat embarrassed the secular Humanist-dominated "educational and publishing establishment" with a book he called *Icons of Evolution* that showed how biology textbooks routinely promote evolution using bogus "evidence-icons" such as Ernst Haeckel's faked embryo drawings and the famous "peppered months of the 19th century English industrial cities." Critics complained that Wells had merely gathered up a handful of innocent errors and blown them out of proportion.

So, in a 2017 follow up book, *Zombie Science*, Wells asked a simple question: If they were just innocent textbook errors, why do so many of them still persist more than a decade later? He wrote:

> Science has enriched our lives and led to countless discoveries but now it is being corrupted. Empirical science is devolving into zombie science, shuffling along unfazed by opposing

evidence. Discredited icons of evolution rise from the dead while more icons—equally bogus—join their ranks. Like a B horror movie they just keep coming! Zombies are make-believe, but zombie science is real—and it threatens not just science, but our whole culture.

The late Stephen Jay Gould was Professor of Geology at Harvard and the curator for invertebrate paleontology in that university's Museum of Comparative Zoology. He was at Harvard from 1967 until his death in 2002. As of 2002 he had published 22 books. He was also America's greatest communicator of evolutionary ideas to the ordinary laymen, which he accomplished through more than 300 essays in *Natural History* magazine between 1974 and 2001. But even Gould spoke out against the zombie science that fills school books. Between 1997 and 2000, evolutionist scientists Michael Richardson and Stephen Jay Gould published articles in *Anatomy and Embryology, Natural History,* and *Science* that criticized Ernst Haeckel's famous 19th Century "embryo drawings" for the fakes that they were because 100 years later textbooks were still teaching that human embryo development is a recapitulation in the womb of evolution from animal ancestors. In *Natural History*, March 2000, Gould wrote that we should be "astonished and ashamed by the century of mindless recycling that has led to the persistence of these drawings in a large number, if not the majority, of modern textbooks." The reason that Haeckel's embryo drawings became an icon of evolution is because, according to evolution, everything, including humans, descended from one common ancestor. Darwin's most famous book was *On the Origin of Species by Means of Natural Selection or the Preservation of Favoured Races in the Struggle for Life.* But evolution theory also embraces his other book that applied his theory to the origin of the human species, *The Descent of Man.* Evolutionists really wanted Haeckel's drawings to be true to the point that they believed they were, contrary to all evidence.

In recent years the teaching that human embryo development is a recapitulation in the womb of evolution from animal ancestors condemned by Gould and others still haunts. For example, Jerry Coyne is a biologist with a Harvard Ph.D. and is one of America's most famous living promoters of evolution and its zombie icons. He is currently a professor emeritus at the University of Chicago's Department of Ecology and Evolution where he had been for many years. In 2009, Coyne wrote a best-selling book, *Why Evolution is True*, and has a website and blog of that name. In that book he wrote that

> Each vertebrate undergoes development in a series of stages, and the sequence of those stages happens to follow the evolutionary sequence of its ancestors ... all vertebrates begin development looking like embryonic fish because we are all descended from a fishlike ancestor.

In the mid-1970s my wife debated a representative of Planned Parenthood at a local high school. During her presentation she showed slides of human fetal development. After the presentation a girl came up to her in tears and explained that she had had an abortion. She had been shown pictures and told that at her stage, it was a fish.

Donald Prothero, who has a Ph.D. from Columbia, has taught at universities such as Cal Tech and Columbia, and as of 2017 was a research assistant at the Natural History Museum of Los Angeles County. He is known as a specialist in mammalian paleontology. In his 2013 textbook, *Bringing Fossils to Life,* he featured Haeckel's original drawings with this caption:

> Embryos of different vertebrates at comparable stages of development (top row) are strikingly similar in every group

In *Zombie Science*, Wells cited even more recent examples of the undead fraud. *Biology*, by Dr. Sylvia Mader and Dr. Michael Windelspecht is in its 13th edition. It is a traditional, comprehensive biology book promoted as suitable for a one or two semester course. The book centers on the evolution and diversity of organisms. In the 2016 edition there is a re-drawn version of Haeckel's embryos, accompanied by the statement, "All vertebrates inherit the same developmental pattern from their common ancestor, but each vertebrate group now has a specific set of modifications to its original ancestral pattern."

Wells cites other recent textbooks that repeat the same theme of descent and recapitulation from ancestral patterns but omit the drawings: a 2014 edition of *Biology* by Raven and Johnson and a 2014 edition of *Biology* by Miller and Levine.

Is it any wonder that in a 2019 survey Pew Research found that 82% of U.S. adults and 87% of U.S. adult Catholics believed that humans evolved from animals? (In a 2014 survey Pew found that only 43% of Evangelicals believed that nonsense). In a debate of sorts via Facebook, a Catholic general practitioner once ridiculed my skepticism of evolution with this debate closer: "You, obviously, have never studied embryology." I think she thought Haeckel's embryo drawings were real.

Jonathan Wells' books have examined other zombies, such as transitional fossils, that haunt textbooks. School children are taught Darwin's 19th century "explanation" of how one species evolved into other species through mutations and natural selection over millions of years. If that is a fact, there should be fossils of the intermediate forms between species. If they existed, they would be known as transitional fossils. Darwin himself predicted these but expressed concern in *Origin of Species*…that to date none had been found. The sudden appearance of fully formed animals with no ancestors and no intermediate forms did not accord with his theory of gradual change. One might think that Darwin gained more conviction regarding his theory, especially as the years went by and he published six editions.

However, far from being a definitive work, the *Origin* is saturated with conjecture. In the final 1876 printing of the 1872 sixth edition, Darwin employed the word "may" 642 times, "if" 493 times, "might" 203 times, "probable" or "probably" 182 times, "tend" or "tendency" 153 times, "suppose(d)" 141 times, "perhaps" 63 times, "no doubt" 58 times, "I believe" occurs 58 times, and "I think" 43 times, and so on. Yet Darwin's disciples hold a belief in the fact of evolution with the zeal that only their non-theistic religion can inspire.

The transitional fossils predicted but not yet found were called "missing links" because of the assumption they actually existed somewhere. The fossils known in Darwin's time showed fully-formed individuals although some were subjects of further debate. Some were thought to be of something that had become extinct and some were the same as living things of his era. Darwin explained that transitional fossils hadn't been found because relatively few fossils had been found. According to Darwin, the reason so few had been found was because the earth's crust had been formed by natural processes such as volcanoes, ice movement, wind, rain and erosion. That was the 18$^{th}$ Century uniformitarian theory of geology that has become today's standard. It replaced the catastrophic theory regarding the Earth's crust based on Noah's Flood. Uniformitarian theory projects the age of the earth to be billions of years. Under those natural conditions, nature would work against a dead organism becoming fossilized. For example, dead animals would be eaten by other animals or birds and their bones would be scattered. If they got buried before they had been picked over, the effects of wind, rain, floods, etc. could uncover them.

When archeology became a much more systematic discipline in the late 19th century and became a widely used tool for historical and anthropological research in the 20th century, more fossils than Darwin ever imagined were unearthed. Millions of fossils have been found. The world's museums are full of fossils. For example, between 1909 and 1915 the Smithsonian Museum collected over 65,000 specimens, many very well preserved, from a site in British Columbia known as the Burgess Shale. These mostly sea creatures are found at 7,500 feet up in the Canadian Rockies. These complex animals had apparently "risen" suddenly, distinct and fully formed, with nothing by way of ancestor forms. Other massive deposits of fossils, distinct and fully formed from the same so-called Cambrian geologic age, were discovered in the mid-1980s in southern China. The "Chengjiang Fossils" are an even greater variety, including soft-body animals, than the Burgess Shale.

All of the scientists who have pursued the quest for the "missing" fossils know that this is a major problem to the theory. Many candidate transitional fossils and human ancestors have been suggested over the years, often with a big splash in the popular media, such as the near hysteria surrounding a fossil consisting of bone fragments representing 40% of a female skeleton found in Ethiopia in 1974 and said to be in the same "tribe" as humans. Technically known as Australopithecus, the fossil was called "Lucy" by its discoverer.

Lucy became a household name at the time. It was early 1979 when TIME magazine crowned her a "front-page celebrity" after "her" discoverer Johanson announced that Lucy was a specimen of *Australopithecus afarensis*, said to be (by Johanson) a whole different species from those previously known *Australopithecus* examples. Johanson said she dated to a period before hominids split into the brand that led to us and the one that led to extinction. "The implications, says Johanson, are profound," TIME noted. "First, the old notion that man became bipedal as his brain grew is certainly false: Lucy was small-brained, but could stand erect. Second, because Lucy is basically so primitive, man may have split from his ape ancestors much later than 15 million years ago, as is commonly supposed."

So, what was Lucy but an ape as her technical name declares and that she was millions of years old and an ancestor of humans is nothing but a theory. In 2015 one of the bones in the Lucy skeleton was found to be that of a baboon, a different animal. In 2016, the Johns Hopkins School of Medicine published a study that confirmed that Lucy was a climber who spent most of her time in the trees and cited another recent study that suggested she died from a fall from a tree.

School teachers at all levels, including college, continue to show students pictures of fossils alleged to be transitional. Professor Jerry Coyne, never to be deterred by the facts, listed many of them in his books and may be blamed in part for the overstatement of the situation. For example, he claimed these to be transitional fossils:

- Ichthyostega (transition between amphibians and reptiles)
- Tiktaalik (transition between fish and amphibians)
- Archaeopteryx (transition between reptiles and birds)
- Ambulocetus (transition between land mammals and whales)

Only the latter three have ever had enough evolutionist support to have become, even briefly, icons of evolution but they are also zombies.

Consider Tiktaalik. Several years ago, the paleontological world heralded the discovery of a fossil called Tiktaalik roseae. Some scientists claimed it as a perfect missing link between fish and amphibians, and so it started appearing in school and university textbooks. However, the discovery of a series of footprints in Poland, made by a four-legged animal, has changed everything. That's because these foot prints were dated according to the same evolutionary ideas at 18 million years older than Tiktaalik. Therefore, from an evolutionary perspective, if four-legged animals existed before Tiktaalik, then Tiktaalik cannot be the transition between fish and four-legged land animals that it was claimed to be. Indeed, these footprints are so significant that they have prompted some scientists to say: "we thought we'd pinned down the origin of limbed tetrapods. We have to rethink the whole thing." Isn't it amazing how just a little bit of new evidence can completely undermine a neat evolutionary story?

As Wells explained. Archaeopteryx is a fossil discovered two years after Darwin first published *Origin of Species...* in 1859.

> A fossil bird was discovered in Germany that had teeth, a long lizard-like tail, and claws on its wings. Its discoverer named it Archaeopteryx ('ancient wing'). Since Archaeopteryx had features of reptiles as well as birds, some people regarded it as the missing link between those two groups and a confirmation of Darwin's theory. In 1998, anthropologist Pat Shipman wrote [in his book *Taking Wing*] that Archaeopteryx is an 'icon of evolution', a holy relic of the past that has become a powerful symbol of the evolutionary process itself. It is the First Bird.

But Wells points out, "there are too many differences between Archaeopteryx and modern birds for the latter to be descendants of the former." He cites evolutionary paleontologist Larry Martin whose article "The relationship of Archaeopteryx to other birds" was in the collection of articles published as *The Beginning of Birds* in Germany in 1985. Martin was a professor at Kansas University and curator of the university's Biodiversity Institute for 40 years:

> Archaeopteryx is not ancestral of any group of modern birds. [Instead it is] the earliest known member of a totally extinct group of birds.

Wells commented that "if animals evolved in a branching-tree pattern, as Darwin believed, then Archaeopteryx was at the end of a long dead branch." Wells asked, "If Archaeopteryx was not the ancestor of modern birds, what was?" He then provided the

78

conflicting opinions of evolutionists themselves. Berkley's Kevin Padian believes birds evolved from dinosaurs. The other opinion, led by North Carolina University's Alan Feduccia, is that birds evolved from a very different group of extinct reptiles.

The dino-bird faction proclaimed itself the "scientific consensus." "Science says" birds are dinosaurs. But Feduccia's contingent hasn't agreed. When a fossil of a dinosaur was discovered in China in 1996 with tiny fibers on it, the dino-bird group called those fibers protofeathers and the animal was proclaimed a "feathered dinosaur." Feduccia and his colleagues held that those tiny fibers were not feather-like at all but collagen, a skin protein, and published that opinion in the *Proceedings of the Royal Society of London B* in 2007. Feduccia followed that in his 2012 book, *Riddle of the Feathered Dragons*, by declaring that "Contrary to popular belief there is no evidence of protofeathers from any Chinese fossils."

Wells provided more of the dueling opinions of eminent evolutionists but I'll leave it where he left it. He pointed out that the

> fossil bird discovered in China apparently predated Archaeopteryx so it is not even the oldest bird, much less the ancestor of modern birds. Meanwhile, both sides of the dino-bird controversy must invent ghost lineages to connect the fossils with each other. Neither side has found the [supposed] ancestor of modern birds. But one thing is for sure: Archaeopteryx is not it.

But the bona fide disagreements published in the scientific literature are of no consequence to the authors and publishers grinding out expensive new textbooks for the public schools to buy. The previously mentioned 2014 *Biology* by Raven and Johnson still called Archaeopteryx "the first bird." Dr. Donald Prothero's 2013 *Bringing Fossils to Life* still calls Archaeopteryx "a missing link" between reptiles and birds. And the students believe it.

The difference between what is taught in school as a fact and that which is only speculation argued over by academic scientists was discussed by Dr. Stephen Meyer in his 2013 *New York Times* best-seller, *Darwin's Doubt: The Explosion of Animal Life and the Case for Intelligent Design*. Meyer explored every theory of biological evolution by an extensive review of the books and papers published by evolutionary biologists. Meyer quotes them and shows why their theories can't explain the source of the information contained in living things. New discoveries by experimental scientists, not only in genetics but in other areas as well, have brought into question the evolutionary dogma. There is enormous disparity between popular representations of the status of the theory and its actual status as indicated in peer-reviewed technical journals. Dr. Meyer noted that

> Evolutionary biologists will acknowledge problems to each other in scientific settings that they will deny or minimize in public, lest they aid and abet the dreaded "creationists" and others they see as advancing the cause of unreason…It is an understandable, if ironic, human reaction, of course, but one that in the end deprives the public of access to what scientists actually know. It also perpetuates the impression of evolutionary biology as a science that has settled all the important questions at just the time when many new and exciting questions about the origin of animal form, for example are coming to the fore.

The other "transitional fossil" on Dr. Jerry Coyne's list that has the status of an icon of evolution concerns the whale. Coyne cites Ambulocetus as the transition between land mammals and whales.

Practically every school child has been taught that millions of years ago a land animal took to the sea and because it didn't use its legs, the legs gradually disappeared. The "proof" for that story is that whales have some small pelvic bones where it is assumed the legs would have been. Since scientists could find no function for those little bones, they pronounced them as "vestiges." In the evolutionists understanding, vestigiality is the retention during the process of evolution of genetically determined structures that have lost some or all of their ancestral function in a given species. In years past, evolutionary science has pronounced hundreds of features in animals and humans as vestiges because they did not know what they were for, so they assumed they were left over from an earlier ancestral species. The term "vestigial" was coined by a 19th Century scientist influenced by Darwin's "use it or lose it" theory. A German, Robert Wiedersheim, in 1893 published a list of 86 human organs that he said had "lost their original physiological significance" and he attributed that to evolution. By 1925, Wiedersheim's list had grown from 86 to 180. Wiedersheim's list was introduced at the famous "Scopes Monkey Trial" by the evolutionist's side with the comment that a human had so many vestigial structures left over from evolution that he was a veritable walking museum of antiquities. The human appendix was for decades an icon of evolution held up as a example of a vestige until it was discovered how important its function was.

As noted above, Dr. Coyne holds that the fossil known as Ambulocetus is a transitional fossil between land mammals and whales. Wells devoted a whole chapter in his book to the supposed evolution of the fossil Ambulocetus as an ancestor of whales. The story he tells goes back to before Ambulocetus was discovered. In 1980, in Pakistan, a small, fossilized land animal was found. The animal looked nothing like a whale or anything similar. However, it was discovered to have a bone in its middle ear that resembled something that had only been found previously in whales, dolphins, and porpoises. The bone is called an "involucrum." Those large aquatic animals are called "cetaceans" from the Latin word cetus which means whale. So, solely because the little land animal had an involucrum (and because the evolutionary story about whales required that they have a land animal ancestor), the little fossil was named Pakicetus (Pakistani whale).

Next came Jerry Coyne's alleged transitional fossil called Ambulocetus. It was discovered by paleontologist Hans Thewissen in Pakistan in 1994. As Wells related it

> The animal had legs that would have enabled it to walk on land like a modern sea lion, but it also had a long tail that would have enabled it to swim like a sea otter. Thewissen and his colleagues interpreted the fossil to be intermediate between land animals and whales, and they named it Ambulocetus natans or "swimming walking whale." A few months later, paleontologist Philip Gingerich and his colleagues discovered a slightly younger fossil in Pakistan they interpreted to be intermediate between Ambulocetus and modern whales. They called their discovery Rodhocetus.

In his 1980 book, *The Panda's Thumb*, Harvard professor Stephen Jay Gould had called the absence of transitional forms "the trade secret of paleontology." He had gained fame in the 1970s for his theory that explained why there were none. With Harvard colleague Niles Eldredge he published that explanation which they called "punctuated equilibrium." According to the new theory, evolution did not take place gradually as Darwin had maintained. Rather, evolution took place in what might be called a series of fits and starts. For example, an animal stayed the same for millions of years and then suddenly an entirely new animal appeared from that old animal with no intermediate forms. Gould's punctuated equilibrium had to be recanted rather quickly because he could postulate no mechanism by which it could take place. So, in 1982 he wrote that:

> And human beings evolved from apelike ancestors whether they did so by Darwin's proposed mechanism or by some other, yet to be discovered.

That is why Gould was absolutely delighted by the fossil discoveries of Thewissen and Gingerich in 1994. Wells recorded Gould's delight:

'The embarrassment of past absence has been replaced by a bounty of new evidence' announced Stephen Jay Gould and 'by the sweetest series of transitional fossils an evolutionist could ever hope to find.' According to Gould, 'this sequential discovery of picture-perfect intermediacy in the evolution of whales stands as a triumph in the history of paleontology. I cannot imagine a better tale for popular presentation of science or a more satisfying, and intellectually based, political victory over lingering creationist opposition.'

To which Wells added the commentary "So 'walking whales' became an icon of evolution."

Wells then devoted the next 12 pages of his book to the scientific controversies in ensuing years as the findings of Thewissen and Gingerich were subjected to peer review. Both Thewissen and Gingerich participated in the discussions and even discovered additional fossils that questioned their original interpretations. For example, a total of seven fossils were arranged in presentation as intermediate stages of an animal that evolved into the blue whale. The first five were fossils of land animals. The controversy then got pretty funny. A fossil that was named Indohyus was discovered to have an involucrum. But it was never considered to be a cetacean. It was classified in an order of land animals that included pigs, hippopotamuses, giraffes, antelopes, sheep, and cattle. Thewissen himself raised the question. Wells quoted him:

> Until now, the involucrum was the only character occurring in all fossil and recent cetaceans but in no other mammals. Identification of the involucrum in Indohyus calls into question what it is to be a cetacean. It requires that either the concept of the Cetaceabe expanded to include Indohyus or that the involucrum cease to characterize cetaceans.

Thewissen and colleagues argued that the involucrum should no longer be used to characterize cetaceans. Wells pointed out the absurdity: "the involucrum is diagnostic of cetaceans, except when it isn't." Where did that leave the little land animal fossil known as the Pakistani whale?

In fact, where did that leave the other four land animals in what Gould had called "the sweetest series of transitional fossils an evolutionist could ever hope to find?" Wells suggested that instead of calling them cetaceans, why not just call them what they were: amphibious land animals like otters and sea lions that spend part of their lives in water.

Wells devoted the rest of that chapter to a detailed biological description of the amazing design of whales that when read can only increase conviction that they were made, not evolved. It is beyond the scope of this book to repeat any of that amazing detail so I'll just close the discussion of the "walking whale zombie" with this factoid. A September 8, 2014, release from the University of Southern California disproved the "whales lost legs" theory. The university published a story on its website titled, "Whale Sex: it's all in the hips." In the article, it announced

> New research turns a long-accepted evolutionary assumption on its head – finding that far from being just vestigial, whale pelvic bones play a key role in reproduction.

And now that they are shown to be necessary, what evidence is there that they are vestigial of anything?

Scientifically dead or debunked theories covered in Well's first book, *Icons of Evolution*, written in 2000 include zombies still walking around in modern textbooks and evolutionary books in the stacks of libraries, including my town's public library. Following are examples of zombie icons.

The 1953 Miller-Urey experiment that is said to have proved life can come from non-life is false. Darwin suggested in 1871 that the original spark of life may have begun in a "warm little pond, with all sorts of ammonia and phosphoric salts, light, heat, electricity, etc. present, so that a protein compound was chemically formed ready to undergo still more complex changes." (We now know that water forms a chemical barrier to the formation of chains of nucleotides such as RNA and DNA.) Darwin's speculation is the origin of the "primordial soup" explanation for the beginning of life found in so many school textbooks and nature programs on PBS. The Primordial Soup Hypothesis was resurrected in 1936 by Russian chemist A. I. Oparin. He proposed how it could have happened if conditions on the Earth back then (whenever back then was) were different than they were at present. Among other things, the proposed soup had to be in an oxygen-free atmosphere. The beauty of that speculation from the evolutionist view point is that it can be told to children without any need to prove it. And it can't be disproved.

In 1952, a graduate student, Stanley Miller, and his professor tested Oparin's idea by mixing water and three gases in an oxygen-free environment, ran electricity through the mix and produced two amino acids. These are not alive but are chemical compounds integral to protein. That was the famous Miller-Urey experiment. It is still in textbooks published in 2014. The fact is that nothing has changed in "origin of life" science since 1952 except the intensity of the propaganda. Take a look at this video where a highly-accomplished scientist explains the status of the research. If you don't have time to watch the whole video, advance it to the 11-minute mark and watch a few minutes.
https://www.youtube.com/watch?v=zU7Lww-sBPg&list=PLR8eQzfCOiS3wfVsVizCzTu9k8zfNOT58&index=6&t=0s
Anyone who reads Stephen Meyer's 2013 *Darwin's Doubt* will learn how and why the origin of life is the "Achilles heel" of the whole evolution fable. For more on "life from a test tube" see
https://evolutionnews.org/2019/01/latest-acts-in-the-origin-of-life-circus/

Darwin's Tree of Life concept is found not only in textbooks but in "pop science" distributed by PBS. It's a branching diagram purporting to show the descent with modification of all living things from a common ancestor. It communicates an impressive story with no evidence to connect the trunk, limbs, and branches. An article in *Scientific American*'s September 2014 Special Evolution Issue provided an article "The Human Saga: Evolution Rewritten" that said "awash in fresh insights, scientists have had to revise virtually every chapter of human history." The scientists to whom the article refers are not empirical scientists; they are "pre-historic" scientists who dig up fossils and make interpretations according to *a priori* strictures. Those strictures require that human descent from animals is a fact. The article features the usual artist drawing of the supposed "Human Family Tree" of skull fragments, all distinct with no transitional forms, and this commentary on that imagined "tree."

> With relatively few fossils to work from, scientists' best guess was that they all could be assigned to just two lineages, one of which went extinct and the other of which ultimately gave rise to us. Discoveries made over the past few decades have revealed a far more luxuriant tree, however-one abounding with branches and twigs that eventually petered out. This newfound diversity paints a much more interesting picture of our origins but makes sorting out our ancestors from the evolutionary dead ends all the more challenging, as paleoanthropologist Bernard Wood explains in the pages that follow.

Homology of Vertebrate Limbs is a zombie that teaches that certain similarities in limb bones of various animals with backbones proves they all descended from a common ancestor. According to evolutionary teaching, effectively communicated to students by pictures, homology is the existence of shared ancestry between a pair of structures, or genes, in different taxa. A common example of homologous structures that evolutionists picture is the forelimbs of vertebrates, where the wings of bats, the arms of primates, the front flippers of whales, and the forelegs of dogs and horses are all said to be derived from the same ancestral tetrapod structure. Even though there are no transitional fossils, their similarities are regarded as undeniable evidence of descent with modification, and they appear in almost every educational textbook promoting evolution. Disproof includes the observation that digit development can be different in amniotes and amphibians (e.g. humans and frogs) and that the forelimbs grow from different embryonic segments (somites) in different species (e.g. newt, lizard and man). If descent with modification were the correct explanation for common forelimb design, we would expect the forelimbs to develop in similar ways and from the same parts of the embryo.

"Darwin's Finches" and Darwin's voyage on the HMS Beagle that took him to the Galapagos Islands where he collected some birds is often the iconic beginning chapter of the evolution story. Actually, Darwin didn't know much of anything about birds. When he got back to England in 1837, he gave the dead specimens of birds he collected to a bird expert, John Gould, who proclaimed that the finches represented 12 distinct species based on the size of their beaks. As reported in the April 2015 edition of evolutionary science magazine, *Discover*, 21$^{st}$ Century science utilizing DNA indicates that none of the Galapagos Island "species" are distinct. Robert Zink of the U. of Minnesota's Museum of Natural History is an ornithologist who said that sequences of their nuclear and mitochondrial DNA show little variation, and none of the telltale signs that suggest distinct species. Zink said it makes more sense to classify the birds as a single species of ground finch with ecologically-driven variation. (The changes in the beak sizes, are "horizontal" within the species; there is no "vertical" descent.)

Four-winged fruit flies produced in the lab by causing a mutation are another zombie used as evidence that DNA mutations, given enough time, could have produced the large-scale differences that led to the various species. That story was told to my grandson by his 5th grade teacher in a private Catholic school that advertises its academic excellence. What the teacher didn't tell him (because she had been taught that same tale I suppose) was that they couldn't fly because they had not the necessary muscles under their wings. And they couldn't reproduce themselves.

Fossil Horses is a set of fossils once used by evolutionists to show that evolution proceeds in a straight line. A sketch showing the supposed evolution of the horse has appeared in nearly every textbook dealing with evolution. A significant problem surfaced when creationist Lou Sunderland observed (in *Darwin's Enigma,* 1998) that mounted specimens in the American Museum of Natural History intended to show the straight line of evolution showed an impossible irregularity of rib pairs. Subsequently it was determined that the fossils were from at least three distinct animals. In modem decades, the tree of horse evolution has been refuted and abandoned, in professional circles at least, but the "zombie" still appears in many publications.

Peppered Moths are an icon familiar to every public-school educated student. Wells relates that the story began when in the 19th century industrialization of England, peppered moths went from being mostly light-colored to being mostly dark-colored. That effect was dubbed "industrial melanism." A biologist theorized that the change occurred because dark moths were better camouflaged on the soot-darkened trees from birds that preyed on moths. It was considered an example of survival of the fittest through natural selection. More than fifty years later, in 1959, the theory was tested by a British physician, Bernard Kettlewell, who released marked light and dark moths into polluted and unpolluted woodlands. He recaptured some of the marked individuals and noted that the proportion of light moths increased in the unpolluted woods and the proportion of dark moths increased in the soot-stained woods. He published his results in *Scientific American* as "Darwin's missing evidence," and peppered moths became the classic example of natural selection in action. i.e., an icon. Even if it were true, the story had nothing to do with Darwin's claim that new species, organs, and body plans were produced by unguided evolution. They were still moths. The story was featured in all biology textbooks, usually with a photograph of light and dark moths resting on light and dark tree trunks. Fast forward another couple of decades to 1980. Researchers discovered that peppered moths don't usually rest on tree trunks. They mostly rest hidden in the higher branches of trees. Further, it was found, peppered moths rarely fly in the daytime. So, by releasing his moths onto nearby tree trunks, Kettlewell had created an unnatural situation. According to Judith Hooper's research for a 2002 book, *Of Moths and Men*, the textbook photographs had been staged, often with dead moths pinned or glued in place. There's more to the moth research in subsequent years but those are the essential facts of the story. Peppered moths are still peppered moths.

The Geologic Column which appears in all of the textbooks naming rock strata, asserting the age of the strata, and the age of the fossils found in that strata exists nowhere except in the textbooks. To actually see 3 or 4 types of strata named in the Geologic Column, one might have to travel over most of the Western United States. The strata in the mythical Geologic Column are not all in one place. The estimate of the age of any particular strata starts with the assumption that evolution is a fact. The age of the strata is determined by the assumed age of "index" fossils (determined by the evolutionary timeline of decent by modification) found in it. Once that strata has been dated by the index fossils, then any other fossils found in that strata are dated by the age of the strata. It is a classic example of the circular reasoning that fools nearly everyone into believing the Earth is very old. It's a brilliant piece of deception. Sedimentary strata can be laid in hours and "old" strata are often found on top of "younger" strata based on the "known" ages of fossils found in them.

The "Ultimate Icon" is the artist conception drawing familiar to everyone. It begins with perhaps a chimpanzee on the left followed by maybe a gorilla to the right of it. Then there is usually something walking semi-upright, hunch-backed and with a very hairy head. Next comes a very wild- looking human carrying a club followed at last by a man who looks like Tarzan. It is "scientifically" supported by a hypothetical fossil lineup in which it is alleged that the one on the left is the ancestor of the one to the right of it. I already explained the hype about "Lucy," the little tree climber. In 2009, there was another burst of hype about a fossil nicknamed "Ida," after the discoverer's daughter. It was said to be the missing link between humans and lower animals. A 2-hour documentary about "Ida" was shown on TV. A few months later, after other paleontologists studied it, an article in the science journal, *Nature*, declared "Ida" was related to lemurs, not humans. Also, in 2009 there was 15 minutes of fame for "Ardi." The "beat goes on" with fossil finds in 2010, 2013, and 2015 that were well-discussed in paleontology journals, all more or less claiming to be some sort of a link to humans, but eventually with peer-review the claims melted. The April 2019 *Acts & Facts* article "Recent Humans with Archaic Features Upend Evolution," summed up the present situation as follows:

> As things stand, the so-called fossil record of human evolution is still nothing but a collection of apes and humans with no transitional forms linking the two groups. This inconvenient fact was the subject of a 2016 Royal Society research paper bearing the provocative title "From Australopithecus to Homo: the transition that wasn't." Numerous studies have shown that the Australopithecines are extinct apes with many chimp-like anatomical traits. Homo is the human genus that includes all of us modern folks among with

our assumed archaic ancestors. In the Royal Society paper, the researchers bluntly state:

'Although the transition from Australopithecus to Homo is usually thought of as a momentous transformation, the fossil record is virtually undocumented.'

https://www.icr.org/article/11255/

Hugh Owen of the Kolbe Institute for the Study of Creation has made an observation about this most familiar icon of evolution that Catholic evolutionists might ponder:

Many people today object that Moses and the ancients could not have understood the complexities of evolutionary science and that this is why God allowed them to believe the fanciful fairy tale of fiat creation. But it is easy to refute this preposterous claim by simply reflecting on the familiar icon of human evolution - the all but omnipresent image of a common ancestor of chimps and humans evolving into an upright human being... In reality, the evolutionary icon does not correspond to any solid scientific evidence in paleontology, genetics, or any other branch of natural science. Moreover, one does not need to know anything about natural science to understand what the evolutionary icon is saying. One does not even need to know that $2 + 2 = 4$ to understand it. So, the whole idea that Moses and the ancients were too simple to understand evolution is absurd. If God had used a natural process, like mutation and natural selection, to evolve the bodies of the first human beings, He could easily have shown this icon to Moses.

Hollywood has caused some people to believe in the ape to human icon. For example, in fantasies in the genre of "Rise of the Planet of the Apes" computer graphics are used to show apes possessing many human-like qualities. But one of the subtler tricks involves "the whites of their eyes." Monkeys and apes don't have them. The "sclera" is the white part of a human eye. In monkeys and apes it is brown or black. By making their sclera white, Hollywood makes their eyes look human and "knowing." The evolutionary journal *National Geographic* has been using that trick for years. For a perfect illustration of that evolutionary wishful thinking-faux science, google this: This Face Changes the Human Story, But How? National Geographic. What comes up is a hyped-up article about fossils found in 2015 that enjoyed the "15 minutes of fame" that "Ida" and "Ardi" had. The very long article leads with "Scientists have discovered a new species of human ancestor deep in a South African cave, adding a baffling new branch to the family tree." While the paleontologists who have been evaluating those fossils since 2015 have made no such claim, Jamie Shreeve, who authored the article, stated that in fact the fossil is our ancestor. Shreeve has parlayed his B.A. in English from ultra-liberal Brown into an extremely successful career writing books and articles on such "fossil fiction" for popular consumption. How many schools have *National Geographic* in their library? How many teachers use it to supplement their teaching of evolutionary "science?" At the top of the article is a large colored picture of the typical simian with human features and white sclera. Underneath the picture in small print it says

> While primitive in some respects, the face, skull, and teeth show enough modern features to justify H. naledi's placement in the genus Homo. Artist Gurche spent some 700 hours reconstructing the head from bone scans, using bear fur for hair.

That sort of propaganda through full-blown artist conception drawings based on fossil fragments has been in the textbooks and popular literature since at least the discovery of the human skull, canine tooth, and doctored orangutan jawbone that became the Piltdown Man fraud in 1912. Shreeve's article also contains the typical "out of Africa" drawing by the same artist that shows a fully-erect gorilla with white sclera, a very primitive black man in a thong, and a black man in a thong like we used to see in pseudohistorical Hollywood adventure movies like "King Solomon's Mines" that featured near-naked tribesmen indigenous to Africa. That conceptualizes the racial superiority of whites that Darwin promoted in his famous *On the Origin of Species by Means of Natural Selection or the Preservation of Favoured Races in the Struggle for Life*. The racial prejudice against blacks as "less evolved" was throughout much of the 20th century justified on such "scientific" grounds. The Discovery Institute produced a documentary called "Human Zoos" that shows how African people were exhibited in cages as subhuman specimens in the evolutionary process. Anyone unfamiliar with that shameful history must google "human zoos with African people."

Monkey Genes are central to another iconic story. The claim that surfaced in 1975 and found its way into the textbooks is that "we share 99% of our genetic sequence with chimpanzees." That really sounds important, but it is not. The explanation of why it is not important is too technical for the level of this book. Anyone interested can go to https://www.icr.org/article/separate-studies-converge-human-chimp-dna and learn all that one can absorb.

In his follow-up book, *Zombie Science*, published in 2017, Wells exposed six more icons that are used to mislead and indoctrinate students about evolution. For example, he explains how DNA has become an icon because zombie science attributes far more significance to the DNA molecule than the evidence justifies. He also covers evolutionary blunders such as alleged vestiges and alleged "junk DNA" which have been debunked. For more details about scientific zombies ask your public library to acquire Well's book. I did.

Persons who have gotten this far into this book, and who have never before heard that there is a serious challenge to the "scientific

93

consensus" regarding evolutionary cosmology and biology, may rightly remain skeptical of what I have written. It is reasonable to ask:

> If the theory of evolution is just so much scientific zombie-filled bunk as you have said, how can you explain that it has become accepted as the scientific consensus and sixty-five percent of American adults believe it?

The short answer to that question is that people believe what they have been taught by the American education institutions such as schools and universities and are also affected by cultural influences. The long answer requires an explanation of how Humanist philosophy has dominated America since its founding and how Humanists have both converted and neutralized Catholics. That long answer is in chapter 14 of *Creation, Evolution, And Catholicism*. Dennis Q. McInerny, when he was Professor of Philosophy at Our Lady of Guadalupe Seminary, summarized the conversion of the majority from the biblical paradigm to the evolutionary paradigm through the education system:

> Over the course of the past century and a half, Western society has allowed itself to be convinced by something which, from a strictly scientific point of view, is singularly unconvincing. I speak of the theory of evolution. But if this theory fails to make the grade as serious science, it has managed to succeed spectacularly as a philosophy, a comprehensive worldview, whose presence is pervasive and whose influence is as powerful as it is deleterious. Its invasion of our educational system is complete, and for decades now the nation's youth have been systematically indoctrinated to accept as an unquestionable "fact" what, in fact, is anything but.

The spectacularly successful philosophy to which Professor McInerny refers is secular Humanism which was identified in chapter 4. Beginning with its ascendancy in the universities in the 1920s, it has come to dominate in academia, professional societies, professional journals, book review publications, blogs, websites, and most other outlets that deal with cosmology and biology. "Dissenters" don't get published, hired, promoted, or elected. Their books are not favorably reviewed. For that reason, academics who are skeptical must "keep their head down."

The evolution alliance comprised of schools, universities, and public and private institutions is too powerful for many scientists to combat on their own. The power of the evolution alliance was well-illustrated by an incident in 2004. The editor of a biology journal, a man with a Ph.D. in evolutionary biology and systems biology, incurred a severe penalty for publishing an article that argued that intelligent design could help explain the origin of biological information. The journal was *Proceedings of the Biological Society of Washington* published by the Smithsonian Institution Museum of Natural History, a Federal Government facility whose employees are in the Federal Civil Service with all of the job protection rules that make it virtually impossible to fire anyone.

The article provoked a national controversy. The evolutionist alliance was furious with Richard Sternberg for allowing the article to be peer-reviewed and publishing it. Museum officials removed him from office and transferred him to a hostile supervisor. They tried to get him to resign but when that failed, they demoted him. Yet, the offending article itself drew no rebuttal because of the typical dodge evolutionists use to avoid debate: they didn't want to dignify it by responding.

Today, the "rule of science" enforced in university faculties and by professional organizations such as the American Association for the Advancement of Science is "methodological naturalism" or "methodological materialism." Stephen Meyer explained the rule as follows:

> Methodological naturalism asserts that to qualify as scientific,
> a theory must explain phenomena and events in nature—even

events such as the origin of the universe and life or phenomena such as human consciousness—by reference to strictly material causes. According to this principle, scientists may not invoke the activity of a mind or, as one philosopher of science puts it, any "creative intelligence."

Humanists control the popular media, the science journals, the research grants, the universities, and the public schools. Professor Rodney Stark, a preeminent American sociologist of religion at Baylor University, observed in *Scientific American* that: "There's been 200 years of marketing that if you want to be a scientific person you've got to keep your mind free of the fetters of religion." He further notes that in research universities "the religious people keep their mouths shut," while "irreligious people discriminate." According to Stark, "there's a reward system to being irreligious in the upper echelons [of the scientific community]." Teachers and grant-dependent research scientists who want to remain employed must follow the party line. The lesson taught to Richard Sternberg was not lost on them.

Evolutionists often claim that science is objective and unbiased, while religion (and by extension, creationism) is biased and dogmatic. True science, they claim, is not about ideology. These skeptics downplay the significance of worldviews, and how they control the interpretation of scientific data. Perhaps a "crack" has appeared in that "wall" of opinion. In 2019 a secular peer-reviewed paper written by a team from the NMBU Centre for Applied Philosophy of Science at the Norwegian University of Life Sciences, confronts the importance of worldviews. (Andersen, F., Anjum, R., and Rocca, E., Philosophy of Biology: Philosophical bias is the one bias that science cannot avoid, *eLife 2019*;8:e44929, 13 March 2019, DOI: 10.7554/eLife.44929.)

In this article, the authors make observations that almost all others in the secular science community are afraid to openly discuss. For example, in the abstract they write:

> Scientists seek to eliminate all forms of bias from their research. However, all scientists also make assumptions of a non-empirical nature about topics such as causality, determinism and reductionism when conducting research. Here, we argue that since these 'philosophical biases' cannot be avoided, they need to be debated critically by scientists and philosophers of science. …
>
> Basic philosophical assumptions count as biases because they skew the development of hypotheses, the design of experiments, the evaluation of evidence, and the interpretation of results in specific directions.

The worldview-based shaping of thought and the spreading of Humanist philosophy explains why Humanism became dominant. The corollary is that belief in evolution became the norm because it is the base upon which Humanism rests. No Incarnation, no Christianity; no evolution, no Humanism. When Catholics accept belief in evolution it is not because they have thoroughly investigated the scientific claims. It is because they have accepted the testimony of Humanists regarding their base dogma. Catholics may have received that testimony from a sincere Catholic who received his belief from a previous sincere Catholic but the ultimate source of the testimony was a Humanist. The way that Humanists hired Humanists in the universities also helps explain the homogenous thought of university faculties, even Catholic ones, on the subject of evolution.

The majority of U.S. scientists are not working in a university (or similar), engaged in teaching theoretical cosmology or evolutionary biology. The majority are engaged in producing commercial products or delivering services. Scientists engaged in the commercial world find no use whatever for evolution theory but even so 30 years into their professional careers most of them believe it because that is what they were taught in college; and they have had no practical need to question it. For example, evolutionist Dr. Marc Kirschner, founding chair of the Department of Systems Biology at Harvard Medical School was quoted in the October 23, 2005, *Boston Globe* as having stated:

> In fact, over the last 100 years, almost all of biology has preceded independent of evolution, except evolutionary biology itself. Molecular biology, biochemistry, physiology, have not taken evolution into account at all.

In similar vein, the anti-creationist Larry Witham wrote:

> Surprisingly, however, the most notable aspect of natural scientists in assembly is how little they focus on evolution. Its day-to-day irrelevance is a great 'paradox' in biology, according to a *BioEssays* special issue on evolution in 2000. 'While the great majority of biologists would probably agree with Theodosius Dobzhansky's dictum that "Nothing in biology makes sense except in the light of evolution", most can conduct their work quite happily without particular reference to evolutionary ideas', the editor wrote. 'Evolution would appear to be the indispensable unifying idea and, at the same time, a highly superfluous one.' (Witham, Larry A., *Where Darwin Meets the Bible: Creationists and Evolutionists in America* (hardcover), p. 43, Oxford University Press, 2002)

Evolution contributes nothing tangible to science but that doesn't mean that hoary 19th Century notions can't be used to sell books to the gullible public. Cardiologist Lee Goldman, dean of the College of Physicians and Surgeons, chief executive of Columbia University Medical Center in a 2015 diet book aimed at the general public titled, *Too Much of a Good Thing*, wrote:

> Can't stick to a diet? That's a holdover from when humans roamed the plains and gorged when food was plentiful, storing

the rest as fat for when it wasn't. Anxiety is a descendant of the fight-or-flight response, which kept us alive when faced with a woolly mammoth but is something that we less often need today.

Is that medical science or something he learned in high school? Medical doctors find evolution theory useless because they are more like results-oriented engineers than theoretical scientists. Evolution is a "white elephant"-big and useless. Its only function is to be the "scientific" proof of the origins myth of the Humanist religion. At http://www.dissentfromdarwin.org read the list of over 1000 Ph.D. scientists who have signed the following statement:

We are skeptical of claims for the ability of random mutations and natural selection to account for the complexity of life. Careful examination of the evidence for Darwinian theory should be encouraged.

# Chapter 8
# The War for Souls and Cultural Survival

All of those icons of evolution misrepresent the evidence that professional biologists have known for decades, but like the dead science they are, they just keep shuffling through the education system in one form or another the way zombies that have avoided burial. The reason why zombie-filled cosmic and biological evolution instruction is aggressively pressed on school children was previously explained. They are the formally-affirmed foundational dogmas of the non-theistic religion that dominates our post-Christian culture, namely, secular Humanism. The Humanist worldview and the confidence Humanists exude as they steamroll Christians, is based on two affirmations of their faith, evolutionary cosmology and biology, that they have taught the majority of Catholics to accept, at least implicitly. The evidence that children are leaving in droves because instruction at school in those dogmas creates a perceived conflict with religion has been "stacked and catalogued." Priests and parish Directors of Religious Education can't just keep doing the "same old, same old" that has failed for the last 50 years. Catholic apologetics needs to implement paragraph 282 of the *Catechism of the Catholic Church*. The creation doctrines that the spokesmen for the Church seem to have forgotten or misplaced must be taught again. And taught with reason based on the 21st Century natural science that refutes those bogus 19th Century theories.

We need to break free to save our children and our Christian culture because if the non-believers comprised of Humanists, agnostics, atheists, and "nones" that include former Catholics become the majority in this country, the social and political consequences will be frightening. Look how they dominate Federal and many state governments, pass immoral laws and control our freedom to travel, assemble, speak, and disagree. That stuff is not politics; it is Humanist religious rage. Censorship and the cancel culture are not the product of Christian teaching or belief. Look at the blatant hypocrisy in our public culture that those involved don't acknowledge or even recognize.

According to Pew Research, in the 2018 midterm elections, 70% of the "nones" voted for a Democrat. Anyone who even follows politics casually ought to know that is no longer the Party that one's Catholic grandfather or dad supported. In the 2020 election 1 of 10 eligible voters was from Gen Z and you know the result. In April 2015, Pat Buchanan succinctly described what that rapidly-increasing demographic of zealous non-theists had already done to us as they became the dominant culture. In a column titled "The Long Retreat in the Culture War," Buchanan observed that "Christianity, driven out of schools and the public square, is being whipped back into the churches and told to stay there." He recounted how the Humanists start by appealing for tolerance.

> First comes a call for tolerance for those who believe and behave differently. Then comes a plea for acceptance. Next comes a demand for codifying in law a right to engage in actions formerly regarded as debased or criminal. Finally comes a demand to punish any and all who persist in their public conduct or their private business in defying the new moral order.

And so it has gone. That final phase didn't just arrive with the 2020 election or the covid-19 power grab by governors in 2019. Just ask "Jack the baker" who had to go all of the way to the Supreme Court in 2018 to defend himself from Colorado officials who would force him to bake a wedding cake for a homosexual "marriage." Ask the West Point, VA, French teacher who, after 7 years on the job, was fired in December 2018 because he wouldn't refer to a female "transgender" by her preferred male pronouns. He claimed it was against his religion but the 5-member school board was unanimously

101

unimpressed. Buchanan observed that "a Christian majority that had the Faith that created Western civilization behind it rolled over and played dead. Christians watched paralyzed as their country was taken from them."

The October 2018 issue of *Imprimis*, a publication of Hillsdale College, had an article titled "America's Cold Civil War." The author was Charles Kesler. It began:

> Six years ago I wrote a book about Barack Obama in which I predicted that modern liberalism, under pressure both fiscal and philosophical, would either go out of business or be forced to radicalize. If it chose the latter, I predicted, it could radicalize along two lines: towards socialism or towards and increasingly post-modern form of leadership. Today it is doing both.

He went on to illustrate his point with the Bernie Sanders campaign in which young liberals learned to embrace socialism openly and the ascendency of what he called the "quasi-Nietzschean faith in race, sex, and power as the keys to meaning and being." Anyone who paid attention to the policies endorsed by that huge cast of 2020 Democrat Party Presidential nominees beginning in 2019 and follows the Biden Administration ought to know that what Bernie started has become mainstream Democrat policy. What Kesler described as "America's Cold Civil War" is just the latest phase of what others long ago dubbed "the culture war" between the values of traditional Christians and those of the Humanists. As Buchanan noted:

> As the culture war is about irreconcilable beliefs about God and man, right and wrong, good and evil, and is at root a religious war, it will be with us so long as men are free to act on their beliefs."

Populist media commentators such as the late Rush Limbaugh and Tucker Carlson used to search for words to describe the post-truth statements of academics, media pundits, and elected officials leading up to 2020 and all they could come up with was the word "crazy." But those they criticized are often highly-educated in the secular sense and successful in careers. Another explanation is required. I have an explanation that Catholics who believe Church teaching that God is the Author of Scripture might consider. It involves one of St. Paul's epistles. Our present dominant culture attributes our beautiful world to the mindless process of evolution and wallows in moral turpitude. St. Paul, in *Romans* 1, explains that because they deny their Creator otherwise intelligent and well-educated people take positions and say things which cause others to question their lack of common sense. It also provides a plausible explanation for the rise of the homosexual/transgender activity and the support and approval that it receives from the majority of non-homosexuals in our culture:

[18] For the wrath of God is revealed from heaven against all ungodliness and wickedness of those who by their wickedness suppress the truth. [19] For what can be known about God is plain to them, because God has shown it to them. [20] Ever since the creation of the world his eternal power and divine nature, invisible though they are, have been understood and seen through the things he has made. So they are without excuse; [21] for though they knew God, they did not honor him as God or give thanks to him, but they became futile in their thinking and their senseless minds were darkened. [22] Claiming to be wise, they became fools; [23] and they exchanged the glory of the immortal God for images resembling a mortal human being or birds or four-footed animals or reptiles.

[24] Therefore God gave them up in the lusts of their hearts to impurity, to the degrading of their bodies among themselves, [25] because they exchanged the truth about God for a lie and worshiped and served the creature rather than the Creator, who is blessed forever! Amen.

**26** For this reason God gave them up to degrading passions. Their women exchanged natural intercourse for unnatural, **27** and in the same way also the men, giving up natural intercourse with women, were consumed with passion for one another. Men committed shameless acts with men and received in their own persons the due penalty for their error.

**28** And since they did not see fit to acknowledge God, God gave them up to a debased mind and to things that should not be done. **29** They were filled with every kind of wickedness, evil, covetousness, malice. Full of envy, murder, strife, deceit, craftiness, they are gossips, **30** slanderers, God-haters, insolent, haughty, boastful, inventors of evil, rebellious toward parents, **31** foolish, faithless, heartless, ruthless. **32** They know God's decree that those who practice such things deserve to die—yet they not only do them but even applaud others who practice them.

Does anything in the above remind the reader of the state of American culture? And in addition, credible reports and criminal evidence show the homosexual influences from the Vatican down to diocesan chanceries worldwide. The bishop-level homosexual revelations that erupted in the U.S. in the summer of 2018 illustrate the lack of faith in high places. If we really believe that God is the Author of Scripture, wouldn't we work and teach to restore belief in God the supernatural Creator Who acts by His Will, honor Him and thank Him for making the universe for us? How it must offend Him when people believe that humans evolved from animals through a naturalistic process. How it must offend Him when the creatures whom He made in His image and likeness with the gift of an intellect refuse to use it to discern the difference between science and tooth-fairy science. And, as Scripture teaches, "they are without excuse."

# Chapter 9
## Calling All Catholic Intellectuals

Many Catholic intellectuals find a "third way" between the scientific consensus and the text of the Bible. While accepting that "something" turned into "everything" over billions of years, as taught to them in school, they overlay it with the belief that God guided evolution. There is extreme vagueness about what those supernatural interventions were and when they happened. Some Catholics who hold that combination have been taught philosophical proofs for the existence of God and have been told that evolution was the playing out of secondary causes flowing according to Divine Providence from the original "whatever it was" created from nothing "whenever." For them it bridges the gap. Some say that paragraph 36 of *Humani Generis* permitted belief in evolution even though it does not. (See Appendix I.) Since they have reached adulthood and feel their Faith is fully intact, it is practically impossible to convince them that belief in evolution is causing others to lose their Faith. Many "tune out" to objections to evolution, such as the lack of scientific evidence, and other rational arguments. The late highly-published, highly-honored Fr. Stanley Jaki exemplified an intellectual "tune out" to the lack of evidence. In a 1997 article supporting his belief in evolution he wrote of it happening by a "mechanism as yet imperfectly understood." Stripped of its sophistry what he communicated was "by faith we 'know' it is true but we don't know how because nothing proposed actually works." That is as convincing as Harvard professor Stephen Jay Gould's 1982 pronouncement that "human beings evolved from apelike ancestors whether they did so by Darwin's proposed mechanism or by some other, yet to be discovered."

This book is an appeal to intellectuals to reconsider because Catholic children are losing their faith because of "faux science." Social researchers have "stacked and catalogued" that evidence. Because of the privilege of one's education, one has a duty to discover and tell the truth.

One doesn't have to be a scientist to bury zombies. The late Tom Bethell did an excellent bit of spade work. His 2017 book, *Darwin's House of Cards: A Journalist's Odyssey Through The Darwin Debates,* is a modern classic. He exposes evolution as a 19th-century idea past its prime, propped up by logical fallacies, bogus claims, and "evidence" that is disintegrating under an onslaught of new scientific discoveries. His concise yet wide-ranging tour of the flashpoints of modern evolutionary theory clearly reveals the weaknesses of the theory that rarely are exposed in mainstream literature and education, or the media. Bethell gave accounts of his interviews with some of the leading evolutionary scientists of the past half century such as Harvard biologists Stephen Jay Gould, E.O. Wilson, and Richard Lewontin.

Some of those men are "human icons of evolution." They were plentifully published, frequently quoted, and highly respected in the scientific education community. For example, E.O. Wilson was a world-renowned biologist. Bethell wrote that Wilson "grew up a Baptist in Alabama and read the Bible through twice. Then, after studying science, he lost his faith." Although he was a world-renowned researcher and author, he made it a practice to teach biology in a mandatory class for non-biology majors. Thus, Harvard students, when they went out to become leading men in the nation, would have learned enough of the evolution story from "a great authority" to facilitate their non-theism for the rest of their careers.

When the highly-credentialed priest whose lecture was analyzed earlier started his assertion of the Day-Age Theory, he "rhetorically asked, where the Bible says that a day was a 24-hour period as most Protestants believe." Actually, most Protestants do not believe that. According to Pew Research, only slightly more mainline Protestants than Catholics believe they evolved from animals. And, according to Christian Smith's research, their children are being peeled away by "faux science" almost as fast as Catholic children are. The majority of Protestant Bible scholars and science academics engaged in the origins debate are evolutionists. The "Harvard" of Protestant theological training is evolutionist Wheaton College Graduate School. The BioLogos Foundation enjoys enormous financial support in turn from the billion-dollar endowed evolutionist Templeton Foundation. BioLogos advertises that it

> invites the church and the world to see the harmony between science and biblical faith as we present an evolutionary understanding of God's creation. Core Commitments: We embrace the historical Christian faith, upholding the authority and inspiration of the Bible.

If the mission of BioLogos is to encourage mainline Protestants to "keep the faith" it isn't working, as Pew and Barna Research have documented. Watch Evangelicals dispute the teaching of BioLogos "Christians" with theology that is perfectly Catholic:
https://www.youtube.com/watch?time_continue=1168&v=1jRlRyrl80E

I believe that a stereotype of so-called "fundamentalist" Protestants pervades in Catholic higher-education circles. My former pastor occasionally made claims from the pulpit about what "our separated brothers" believe about the Bible and I could only just smile and shake my head. Usually, his remarks were about how they are missing out on so much because they don't have the Holy Eucharist because they refuse to accept the literal meaning of Jesus' "Bread of Life Discourse" in *John* 6. The gospel on *Corpus Christi* Sunday 2019 was Luke's account of the "multiplication of the loaves and fishes" which prefigures the Holy Eucharist. He gave a great sermon about the Real Presence including a recitation of some of the Eucharistic miracles such as Lanciano. During that sermon he said the "Fundamentalists believe God created the world in 6 days and rested on the 7th; why don't they believe the Bible about the necessity of the Body and Blood?" Yet he doesn't accept that God created the world in 6 literal days as the Bible says and the "interpretation" he has preached is that science tells us the "when" and "how" of origins but only the Church can tell us the "why." I once called him a theistic evolutionist to his face. He just chuckled. Around 2009, in *Opus Dei*'s Washington, DC Catholic bookstore, I perused a new moral theology book written by a priest on the faculty of its well-known Spanish Catholic university. He explained that the only people who didn't believe in an evolutionary interpretation of the Bible were "American fundamentalists."

For over 50 years, since Vatican Council II, there have been Catholic Church sponsored representatives engaging in "ecumenical dialog" with representatives of other bodies, such as Lutherans, to seek areas of theological common ground. Since it is a fact, proved by reams of data collected by social science researchers, that Evangelical children can articulate what they believe and are more likely to keep their faith than Catholic children, it might be useful for Catholic intellectuals to dialog with Evangelical scientist-apologists to seek areas of common ground on *Genesis*. I once took the Headmaster and 4 men who taught at a private Catholic high school to a 2-day seminar given by scientists from the Institute for Creation Research. On the way home they talked about the high quality of the presenters and the enlightening content.

The seminary professors immersed in the "scientific method" of deconstructing their students' belief in the supernaturalism of the Bible may not want to participate in such dialogs but there is nothing preventing any priest who is zealous for souls from participating. I may appear to be engaging in hyperbole about what goes on in some seminaries. Earlier I related what a Diocese of Arlington pastor wrote in "The Catholic Thing" blog about his Bultmann-based seminary scripture instruction in the 1980s. In some places nothing much has changed since the 1980s. In October 2015, a Scripture professor then on the staff at Mt. St. Mary's Seminary in Maryland gave a lecture to a group of laymen in Virginia on the topic of *Genesis* 1-2 that was videoed. It was so bizarre that I did a line-by-line critique of it in *Creation, Evolution, and Catholicism: A Discussion for Those Who Believe.* The lines from that lecture that best illustrate the deconstruction of seminary students' beliefs were:

> Now hear this, this really startles my seminarians when I read this next quote, 'cause for them it is pulling the rug out from under the six days of creation. Listen to this very interesting quote.

A paper he handed out and read from described *Genesis* 1 and 2 as a mish-mash of symbols involving temples real and spiritual. That discussion of *Genesis* 1 and 2, particularly with its emphasis on temple symbolism, had an uncanny resemblance to the scholarship of J.H. Walton, a well-published Protestant author and Professor of Old Testament, who joined the faculty of liberal Protestant Wheaton College around the time the St. Mary's professor was getting his M.A. in New Testament Theology there. While at Wheaton he reverted to Catholicism from which he had strayed for years.

Stacy Trasancos has a Ph.D. in chemistry. She obtained an M.A. in Dogmatic Theology, summa cum laude. from Holy Apostles College and Seminary. She is an adjunct professor of chemistry/theology at Holy Apostles Seminary. In an article published in the *National Catholic Register* she explained that:

> We can say that God created our first parents, as He did all creatures, and that they were highly complex organisms. That description applies whether Adam and Eve began as zygotes with human souls growing in maternal bodies or as naked adults in a garden.

If Adam and Eve or those evolving things were zygotes with human souls growing in maternal bodies, that would make them the first Immaculate Conceptions because they were certainly conceived without Original Sin. And if Adam had a mother, how can we square that with Luke's gospel in which he gives the genealogy of Jesus by naming the fathers all the way back to Adam who he says was "the son of God."? (3: 38)? Did the Holy Spirit "overshadow" some human (or non-human) "maternal" body as in the Incarnation? Further, it is a certain and undisputable teaching of the Church that Eve was made from Adam so she was no zygote in a maternal body. That also tells something about the ignorance of the *NCR*'s editors who published Professor Trasancos' theology fiction. Trasancos is the "science expert" for the package of "educational material" sold to parishes and known as FORMED.

Many highly-credentialed scholars teach seminarians Scripture according to the evolution-based "scientific method" of biblical exegesis, of which the examples above are representative. The bishops who send the young men to those seminaries respect academic credentials. The St. Mary's Seminary professor mentioned above enhanced his M.A. from Protestant Wheaton College with a Ph.D. in New Testament & Early Christianity from Loyola of Chicago, a problematic Jesuit university. Bishops are impressed! Most of the bishops were probably taught and believe the same stuff. As long as the professors have credentials, bishops aren't likely to interfere.

I have no academic credentials but I've taken to heart what I quoted earlier that Leo XIII and St. Pius X said about the destructive effect of belief in evolution. "But," one may object, "that was said at the beginning of the 20th century." Fast forward then to 1950 when Pope Pius XII issued the encyclical *Humani Generis.* The English title of that encyclical is *The Human Race: Some False Opinions Which Threaten To Undermine Catholic Doctrine. Humani Generis* is primarily about the bad philosophy spreading through Catholic institutions of formation because of the uncritical acceptance of evolutionary theory. Pius XII twice named evolution as the problem in the 5th and 6th paragraphs of the encyclical.

> 5. If anyone examines the state of affairs outside the Christian fold, he will easily discover the principle trends that not a few learned men are following. Some imprudently and indiscreetly hold that evolution, which has not been fully proved even in the domain of natural sciences, explains the origin of all things, and audaciously support the monistic and pantheistic opinion that the world is in continual evolution. Communists gladly subscribe to this opinion so that, when the souls of men have been deprived of every idea of a personal God, they may the more efficaciously defend and propagate their dialectical materialism.
>
> 6. Such fictitious tenets of evolution which repudiate all that is absolute, firm and immutable, have paved the way for the new erroneous philosophy which, rivaling idealism, immanentism and pragmatism, has assumed the name of existentialism, since it concerns itself only with existence of individual things and neglects all consideration of their immutable essences.

Some younger persons not familiar with Communism and the antithesis of the Church toward it might miss the significance of the Pope's reference to "Communists" in paragraph 5 above. In 1937, his predecessor, Pius XI, wrote an encyclical, *Divini Redemptoris* (On Atheistic Communism), reinforcing the long-standing Church teaching against that ideology and its connection to evolution.

> The doctrine of modern Communism, which is often concealed under the most seductive trappings, is in substance based on the principles of dialectical and historical materialism previously advocated by Marx, of which the theoricians of bolshevism claim to possess the only genuine interpretation. According to this doctrine there is in the world

only one reality, matter, the blind forces of which evolve into plant, animal and man. Even human society is nothing but a phenomenon and form of matter, evolving in the same way. ... In a word, the Communists claim to inaugurate a new era and a new civilization which is the result of blind evolutionary forces culminating in humanity without God.

In 1950, when Pius XII wrote *Humani Generis*, armies of the NATO Alliance and the Communist Warsaw Pact armies stood eyeball to eyeball at a border of thousands of miles, known as "The Iron Curtain," which ran through Europe and enclosed the eastern part of that continent under Communist rule. No more serious a warning about evolution could have been made in 1950 than to explain how useful it was to the Communists. Pope Pius XII knew where evolutionary theory leads when it undergirds a philosophy. He said that through it "the souls of men have been deprived of every idea of a personal God."

> In fact, not a few insistently demand that the Catholic religion take these sciences into account as much as possible. This certainly would be praiseworthy in the case of clearly proved facts; but caution must be used when there is rather question of hypotheses, having some sort of scientific foundation, in which the doctrine contained in Sacred Scripture or in Tradition is involved. If such conjectural opinions are directly or indirectly opposed to the doctrine revealed by God, then the demand that they be recognized can in no way be admitted.

Fast forward again to the late 1980s. when Cardinal Ratzinger made it pretty plain in those two lectures that I cited that belief in evolution is killing authentic exegesis and philosophy while suppressing the creation doctrines.

There is a small minority of Catholic evolution dissenters or skeptics. These include younger priests such as Fr. Chaberek and older scholars such as Brian W. Harrison, O.S., M.A., S.T.D. But maybe more importantly there are a few lay intellectuals at Catholic colleges or seminaries who are known by what they have published to be skeptical of evolution theory, and may be open to a dialog conference with "young earth creationist" scientists. Those Catholic intellectuals are not scientists but the creation vs. evolution debate is not primarily about science. The science is "zombie science." The debate is about philosophy and biblical exegesis and worldviews. The lectures of Cardinal Ratzinger show evolution to be a philosophical faith principle that has corrupted philosophy and biblical exegesis. Further, acceptance of the foundational dogma of the Humanist religion has crippled Catholic confidence in the public square.

Bad things happen when bad ideas are spread and become fashionable. Our children are being seduced away from their parents' faith. Meticulous social research produced by the decades-long "National Study of Youth and Religion" led by Christian Smith, Professor of Sociology at the University of *Notre Dame*, Director of the Center for the Study of Religion and Society, shows that Catholics are losing their faith because of what they see as a conflict between the Bible and (faux) science. As one of the teens interviewed by Christian Smith during his massive research project put it

> I mean there is proven [scientific] fact and then there is what's written in the Bible—and they don't match up. So it's kinda whatever you wanna believe: there is fact and there is a book, and some people just don't wanna believe the truth [of science].

Catholics are called to be witnesses, the "sign of contradiction." It is scary for an academic to swim against the stream of the "consensus" when it comes to evolution. In the same way that scientists are made to conform to "group think," so also are professors in theology, philosophy and Scripture. Their careers often rest on getting papers

113

published in the right journals. Some academics even object when colleagues at their college get on the "wrong" side of evolution for fear that they will be "tarred with the same brush" and even that could hurt their publishing opportunities.

Many Catholic blogs and other publications express the concern that some intellectuals have about what Pope Francis says and does. Often there is reference to the past and the "good old days" of Benedict XVI. If the traditional authoritative teachings are such favorites with intellectuals who self-identify as "traditional" or "orthodox," they should be defending what Pius X, XI, XII, and Ratzinger-Benedict XVI have said: Evolution undermines Catholicism. There are academics who fear for their reputations if they go against the "academic consensus" on evolution. Fear can paralyze one's conscience. When the sex scandal cover-up regarding bishops erupted in 2018, many of the laity asked: "Why didn't those who knew the truth come forward instead of keeping silent?" "Fear of reprisal" was a common answer. The same question lies before Catholic intellectuals regarding evolution and the authoritative teaching of the popes. If intellectuals fear to teach the truth, who will?

Readers (parents, priests, mature students and others) seeking to understand more about these issues such as evolutionary cosmology, evolutionary biology, theology, philosophy, and the history of the debate, should consider the education resources listed in Appendix II

# Appendix I
## Is Our Lady's Ancestor a Beast?

To even ask the question may seem blasphemous, but that Our Lady descended from an animal is the logical conclusion that Catholics who believe and promote the theory of evolution refuse to acknowledge. Many well-meaning educators have sought to counter the alleged superiority of science over the Bible by embracing the "faux science" at the expense of the Bible to "interpret away" the conflict. Through a combination of scientific ignorance and dissent from the Magisterium on the subject of biblical inerrancy they are promoting cosmic and biological evolution as mainstream as long as one understands that "God did it."

The theory of evolution is that all humans descended from non-humans, that is, that there is biological continuity between animals and humans. That theory, promoted as a fact by the secular "scientific consensus," is the thesis of Charles Darwin's second most-famous book, *The Descent of Man, and Selection in Relation to Sex* first published in 1871. Darwin's second book applied to humans the evolutionary theory developed in his *On the Origin of Species by Means of Natural Selection, or the Preservation of Favoured Races in the Struggle for Life*, published in 1859. According to a study published in 2019 by Pew Research, 87% of Catholics believe humans descended from non-human animals, literally, from beasts.[1] There is no way of escaping the conclusion that if humans descended from animals, so did Our Lady and for that matter, so did Our Lord.

The most common story by Catholics who promote evolution is that "God did it," or "God guided it." The scientific knowledge of those who promote such stories is so superficial they believe that they can "baptize" what is essentially a dogma of the non-theistic religion of secular Humanism[2] and harmonize it with Catholicism. Most Catholic evolutionists don't even have a coherent explanation for what they believe, but here is one story that has circulated in Catholic circles for over half a century. James Fitzpatrick, a man who undoubtedly loved the Church and strove to believe all that it teaches, wrote in his regular "First Teachers" column of January 22, 2015, in the orthodox Catholic newspaper, *The Wanderer*, a commentary that referred to a speech that had recently been given by Pope Francis that concerned evolution:

> I don't know if my experience is typical, but this is the understanding of the Book of *Genesis* that I have been taught since I was in high school in the Bronx in the 1950s. The Marist Brothers who taught me at that time would tell their students that Catholics are free to believe that evolution took place, as long as they understood it to be a process begun by God, and one in which human beings were created when God infused a soul into the evolving creature that became man. This was the same understanding taught to me by Jesuit priests at Fordham in the 1960s.

This belief has never been taught by the Church or held to be true, but, like many falsehoods, it has its origin in a speck of truth that has been distorted into a mountain of error. In 1950, Pope Pius XII issued the last published authoritative teaching on the subject of evolution in his encyclical, *Humani Generis*. The English title of that encyclical is *The Human Race: Some False Opinions Which Threaten to Undermine Catholic Doctrine.* The Pope identified the cause of those "false opinions" in the encyclical's fifth paragraph: evolution.

In paragraph 34, the Pope explained how and why the new opinions conflicted with the constant teaching of the Church. In paragraph 35 he explained that because of the ever-increasing belief in evolution

> ... not a few insistently demand that the Catholic religion take these sciences into account as much as possible. This certainly would be praiseworthy in the case of clearly proved facts; but caution must be used when there is rather question of

hypotheses, having some sort of scientific foundation, in which the doctrine contained in Sacred Scripture or in Tradition is involved. If such conjectural opinions are directly or indirectly opposed to the doctrine revealed by God, then the demand that they be recognized can in no way be admitted.

So, to accommodate those within the Church who were demanding that Catholicism take the claims of science into account, he set up a mechanism for those advocates of evolution to "make their case." In paragraph 36 of the encyclical, the Pope set up a perfectly fair and rational plan for resolving the apparent conflict between evolution advocates and the traditional teaching of the Church. It is this paragraph upon which Catholic promoters of evolution have been basing the false teaching, such as that taught to James Fitzpatrick by Jesuits and others for nearly 70 years, that:

Catholics are free to believe that evolution took place, as long as they understood it to be a process begun by God, and one in which human beings were created when God infused a soul into the evolving creature that became man.

Here is paragraph 36 in its entirety and it is impossible to take from this paragraph the understanding that James Fitzpatrick believed to be true:

36. For these reasons the Teaching Authority of the Church does not forbid that, in conformity with the present state of human sciences and sacred theology, research and discussions, on the part of men experienced in both fields, take place with regard to the doctrine of evolution, in as far as it inquires into the origin of the human body as coming from pre-existent and living matter - for the Catholic faith obliges us to hold that souls are immediately created by God. However, this must be done in such a way that the reasons for both opinions, that is, those favorable and those unfavorable

117

to evolution, be weighed and judged with the necessary seriousness, moderation and measure, and provided that all are prepared to submit to the judgment of the Church, to whom Christ has given the mission of interpreting authentically the Sacred Scriptures and of defending the dogmas of faith. Some however, rashly transgress this liberty of discussion, when they act as if the origin of the human body from pre-existing and living matter were already completely certain and proved by the facts which have been discovered up to now and by reasoning on those facts, and as if there were nothing in the sources of divine revelation which demands the greatest moderation and caution in this question.

Where does that paragraph say Catholics are free to believe in evolution "as long as they understood it to be a process begun by God, and one in which human beings were created when God infused a soul into the evolving creature that became man?" The paragraph says the Church <u>does not forbid discussion</u> of the theory of evolution's claim that the human body evolved from "pre-existent and living matter," i.e., a living non-human creature which, in plain language, would be an animal. What was not opened to even discussion was the origin of the soul. If God infused a soul into a living creature that was conceived by any reproductive process now known to science, and that creature became the first human, it would also be the first Immaculate Conception because it was conceived without Original Sin.

Note that the discussion was not opened to "every Tom, Dick, and Harry." It was opened to persons expert in <u>both</u> natural science and theology. The discussion was to be like a court case in which data and reasoning on the data by expert witnesses are offered by each side in support of its opinions or conclusions to a judge for evaluation and decision:

However, this must be done in such a way that the reasons for both opinions, that is, those favorable and those unfavorable to evolution, be weighed and judged with the necessary seriousness, moderation and measure, and provided that all are prepared to submit to the judgment of the Church, to whom Christ has given the mission of interpreting authentically the Sacred Scriptures and of defending the dogmas of faith.

In the 7 decades since those discussions were not forbidden, did they ever take place? The Pope gave evolutionists the challenge to "put up or shut up" but they have neither put up nor shut up. They just kept doing what he said in the same paragraph that they had already been doing.

Some however, rashly transgress this liberty of discussion, when they act as if the origin of the human body from pre-existing and living matter were already completely certain and proved by the facts which have been discovered up to now and by reasoning on those facts, and as if there were nothing in the sources of divine revelation which demands the greatest moderation and caution in this question.

A Benedictine monk wrote in a letter to this author:

I recently read a passage in *Fundamental Theology* by Guy Mansini, OSB (Catholic University Press, 2018, p. 160) which asserts "According to Pius XII Catholics are entirely free to embrace 'the doctrine of evolution concerning the human body'" with a footnote to *Humani Generis*. One wonders if he even bothered to look at the encyclical.

Is your ancestor an animal or Adam, a specialty made creation who in Luke's genealogy of Jesus, is identified as "the son of God" (3: 38)? Do you accept the tooth-fairy science behind the theory of evolution, just shrug and say "God did it" because you have not the interest or mental diligence to think it through? Catholics used to believe that truth mattered. It does matter whether humans evolved from animals as the "scientific consensus" says or we were specially made to live and glorify God in the universe He has created just for us.

British philosopher Mary Midgley recognized long ago that

> Evolution is the creation myth of our age. By telling us our origins it shapes our views of what we are. It influences not just our thoughts but also our actions in a way which goes far beyond its official function as a biological theory.

Notes

1. https://www.pewforum.org/2019/02/06/the-evolution-of-pew-research-centers-survey-questions-about-the-origins-and-development-of-life-on-earth/?

2. The 1st and 2nd affirmations of non-theistic faith proclaimed in the *Humanist Manifesto I* https://americanhumanist.org/what-is-humanism/manifesto1/

# Appendix II
## Science and Catholicism Resources

*Creation, Evolution, and Catholicism: A Discussion for Those Who Believe* by Thomas L. McFadden addresses science, theology, philosophy, and history of the debate for the non-professional reader (parents, priests, mature students).

**Intellectual Combat: Resistance to Religious Atheism** by Thomas L. McFadden examines the competing ideologies of Catholicism and Humanism. For McFadden's books see www.ScienceandCatholicism.org

*The Doctrines of Genesis 1-11: A Compendium and Defense of Traditional Catholic Theology on Origins* (2007).

*Darwin's Doubt: The Explosive Origin of Animal Life and the Case for Intelligent Design* by Stephen C. Meyer. Very readable for the ordinary non-scientist. *NYT* best seller list in 2013.

*Darwin's House of Cards: A Journalist's Odyssey through the Darwin Debates* (2017) by Tom Bethell is a masterpiece of science, history, and philosophy by a non-scientist. Easy reading.

*Aquinas and Evolution* (2017) by Michael Chaberek. O.P. explains why St. Thomas's teaching on the origin of species is incompatible with evolutionary theory. Readers versed in philosophy will enjoy.

**Foresight: How the Chemistry of Life Reveals Planning and Purpose** (2019) by Marcos Eberlin. Dr. Eberlin is a Brazilian with over a 1000 published scientific articles and this book is chock full of amazing descriptions such as human reproduction, migratory bird navigation, bacteria, bugs and carnivorous plants that demonstrate "foresight" which is another expression meaning intelligent design.

**Spacecraft Earth: A Guide for Passengers** (2017) by Dr. Henry Richter debunks evolutionary cosmology by explaining how rare the Earth is. Easy reading for the non-scientist.

*Zombie Science* (2017) by Jonathan Wells. Easy read for the non-scientist. Debunks dead science still taught as facts in schools.

**Kolbe Center for the Study of Creation** (online at kolbecenter.org) has a vast amount of free reading and great books for sale. This is the website for authentic Catholic creation theology and natural science. Follow also on Facebook.

**The Institute for Creation Research** (online at icr.org) is the premier creation science resource. In addition to so much free information online, ICR sells books and DVDs suitable for all ages. Get *Acts & Facts* a free monthly magazine. Subscribe on the website.

**Creation Ministries International** (online at creation.com) Subscribe to CMI's free daily email science articles and get a creation science education day by day. *This is a super resource.* CMI also publishes a great science magazine, *Creation.*

**The Discovery Institute's Center for Science and Culture** (online at discovery.org/id/) is a comprehensive resource offering much free information. Subscribe and get a free email called Nota Bene. Look at www.evolutionnews.org. Bookmark it.

**The Creation Research Society** is a professional membership organization of scientists and laypersons committed to scientific special creation and a young earth. They publish a great quarterly of scientific importance. creationresearch.org/

**Center for Scientific Creation** (online at creationscience.com/) The comprehensive book on the Flood and the earth's geology called *In the Beginning: Compelling Evidence for Creation and the Flood.* You can read it <u>FREE</u> online.

**Daylight Origins Society**-Creation science in the UK and Ireland www.daylightorigins.com

*******************************************t

**Institute for Science and Catholicism** (ISC) sends copies of books free to priests and seminarians. To support this effort with a tax-deductible donation to ISC use the "donate" button at the bottom of our website's home page. www.scienceandcatholicism.org Read good science articles by "Liking" ISC's Facebook page https://www.facebook.com/scienceandcatholicism/